The COURAGEOUS CHURCH

Standing Boldly for Truth in a Cowardly World

BOB PEARLE

Foreword by Jack Hibbs

Olde Quill Press
Dallas, Texas

The Courageous Church:
Standing Boldly for Truth in a Cowardly World
Copyright © 2026 by Bob Pearle

Olde Quill Press
Dallas, Texas
ISBN: 979-8-9948370-0-9
V03242026SC
Also available in eBook Publication.

Cover images: Concert goer ©dwphotos242; lion @adogslifephoto. Licensed from DepositPhotos.com. Cover Design/Interior Design/Publishing Assistant: Ellen Sallas, theauthorsmentor.com

All rights reserved. No part of this book may be reproduced, stored in a retrieval system, or transmitted in any form or by any means—electronic, mechanical, photocopy, recording or otherwise—without written permission of the publisher, except for brief quotations in printed reviews.

Scriptures quoted in *The Courageous Church* are taken from the following versions: The Holy Bible, King James Version (KJV), public domain. | The Holy Bible, English Standard Version® (ESV®), Copyright© 2001 by Crossway, a publishing ministry of Good News Publishers. Used by permission. All rights reserved. | The New American Standard Bible® (NASB®), Copyright© 1960, 1962, 1963, 1968, 1971, 1972, 1973, 1975, 1977, 1995 by the Lockman Foundation. Used by permission. | The Holy Bible, The New King James Version® (NKJV®), Copyright© 1982 by Thomas Nelson. Used by permission. All rights reserved.

PUBLISHED IN THE UNITED STATES OF AMERICA

PRAISE FOR *THE COURAGEOUS CHURCH*

"Bob Pearle challenges us to use the religious freedom that Charlie Kirk died for. If you want to avoid being spit out because you're lukewarm, read this book. It's an elegantly written challenge to churches to engage the culture."

– Dave Arnott, PhD., Dean of Turning Point USA's Prep Year program

"Pastor Bob Pearle has written a book the Church ignores at its peril. The Courageous Church is a clear, biblical, and urgently needed call for Christians to recover the courage and clarity our moment demands. In a culture increasingly hostile to truth, this book reminds pastors and believers alike that faithfulness—not comfort—has always been the Church's true calling."

– Eric Metaxas, Best-Selling Author of *Bonhoeffer* and *Letter to the American Church*

"Courage isn't optional for the Christian, especially in a cultural moment like this one when so much is at stake. Pastor Pearle's challenge comes from Scripture and history, to be *who* God has called us to be *where* God has called us."

– John Stonestreet, President of the Colson Center

"As I travel the country speaking and preaching, people often ask me, 'Tony, what keeps you up at night?' I think they expect me to name some global threat I've discussed with national leaders. And to be sure—there are plenty of threats in the world today. But the greatest threat to our nation isn't geopolitical. It's a lack of moral courage—the kind of courage that can only be born from deep spiritual conviction and unwavering confidence in the truth of God. Dr. Bob Pearle puts his finger on the real need of this generation: we must rediscover the church's legacy of courage and truth."

– Tony Perkins, President, Family Research Council, host of Washington Watch

"America was birthed by the grace of God and the influence of the church and pastors. Historians have documented that the most influential voices in the founding era were the clergy. As one historian noted, 'There is not a right asserted in the Declaration which had not been discussed by the New England clergy before 1763.' Without the church, and many bold pastors, America never would have come into existence. Sadly, the current crisis in America is because of the lack of leadership from churches and pastors. *The Courageous Church*, by Bob Pearle, is a reminder of why God created the church and what the church and believers must do: *Standing Boldly for Truth in a Cowardly World*. Every pastor and church needs to regain the truths outlined in this book. This is the time for courage."

– Tim Barton, President, WallBuilders

"If we want courageous Christians, we need courageous pastors. From the pulpit to his personal ministry and friendships, Pastor Bob Pearle is a pastor's pastor, uncompromising with the truth, a man of conviction and compassion. He demonstrates how the Word of God intersects with life in this world. It takes courage to speak the truth in an era of lies. Bob's obedience to God's calling over decades of ministry has built a legacy of courage.

Every generation of Christians is faced with challenges. At times we have faltered, and at others we have changed the world. Today, the church faces a choice: retreat, or step out and stand firm for the truth. We hear the echoes down the halls of church history, 'Have I not told you? Be strong and courageous?' But the question remains—how? Bob provides that answer through Scripture, church history, and personal experience. He has lived courageously, and now you hold his wisdom in your hands."

– Lance Cashion, CEO/Founder,
Forge Room Foundation

"This book is a must read that will equip Christian leaders to reclaim the steel-spined conviction that built the early church and can rebuild ours today. Courage is the only virtue that guarantees biblical truth is heard and that faith is championed; courage is needed now more than ever."

– Ryan Helfenbein, Vice President of
Communications and Public Engagement,
and the Founding Executive Director of the
Standing for Freedom Center
at Liberty University

*Dedicated to my wife, Deborah.
My steadfast helpmeet in life and in calling. For more than fifty years of ministry, she has loved me faithfully and prayed without ceasing. A quiet warrior of the soul, she has bombarded heaven on my behalf, and in answer, God has given me strength to stand in the gap when the battle was most fierce.*

*A*cknowledgements

There is an old saying that "many hands make work light," and that is certainly true when bringing a book into print. This process does not happen in isolation but with the cooperative efforts of many talented people.

I want to thank Tony Byrne for his keen eye and excellent work in editing this work. Even with all the great modern tools in publishing there's still no substitute for a sharp human eye to catch the details automation will miss. Tony is that guy.

I also want to express my sincere gratitude to Ellen Sallas, Director of Little Roni Publishers and host of The Author's Mentor website. She has worked her magic on the formatting and coordinated the many moving parts necessary to bring this book to press. She is very gifted in her own right and has been a joy to work with, patiently answering the multitude of questions I sent her way.

I would be remiss if I did not acknowledge Birchman Baptist Church, where I have had the privilege of serving as pastor since January 1998. God has assembled an exceptionally gifted staff, and this faithful congregation has encouraged, supported, and prayed for me throughout the years. While some churches have wavered or accommodated the shifting winds of culture, Birchman has remained steadfast in its commitment to the Word of God and has faithfully followed pastoral leadership.

Finally, I want to acknowledge my sweet wife, Deborah. She is the best cheerleader, and together we have shared a blessed life of ministry.

Table of Contents

Foreword 1
Introduction: When the Church Stood Tall 3

Section I: A Heritage of Holy Boldness (The Historical Church) . 9
    1: Courage in the Early Church 11
    2: The Reformation Fire 19
    3: Courage on the American Soil 29

Section II: The Decline of Courage (The Contemporary Crisis) . 41
    4: The Cowardice of Compromise 43
    5: Diagnosing the Modern Church 51

Section III: The Call to Courage (The Church Today) 65
    6: The Portrait of Courage 67
    7: The Gospel in a Hostile Climate 80
    8: Standing Together Courage in Community 92

Section IV: Fueling the Flame (Where Courage Comes From) . 103
    9: Biblical Foundations for Courage 105
    10: Spiritual Disciplines of the Courageous 114

Conclusion: Will We Be Found Faithful 125
    About the Author 133

Foreword

THERE ARE MOMENTS IN A NATION'S LIFE WHEN the fog lifts and the choices before us become plain. The choices may not be easy, but they are clear. Graduate degrees are not essential to tell the difference between courage and cowardice and conviction or convenience. In these times, the Church is tempted to do what every other institution does, soften the edges, lower the voice, and aim for the middle so nobody gets upset. But the Church of Jesus Christ was never built to be a polished echo of the culture.

The book you're holding is a needed call for believers to wake up, stand up, and speak up; not with arrogance, not with anger, and certainly not with fear. It is a reminder that courage is not a personality trait for a few leaders but biblical courage is simply what obedience looks like even if it costs.

That's why I'm grateful for Bob Pearle and his book, *The Courageous Church*. This is not a book that tries to stir you up to anger. It's a book that seeks to strengthen you into faithfulness. I've known Bob as a faithful pastor and brother who understands what many have forgotten - truth is not negotiable. Truth is not improved by editing it or made more loving by hiding it. In a world that rewards silence and wants to crush conviction, *The Courageous Church* insists that the most loving thing we can do is tell the truth, with humility and compassion and live the truth before a watching world.

If you're a pastor or a Christian leader, this book will challenge you to lead with backbone and tenderness like Jesus did. If you're a Christian trying to raise a family and maintain a Christian witness, this book will remind you that you are not alone and you are not foolish for standing on God's Word.

The Courageous Church is not the Church that never feels fear, but it is the Church that refuses to be ruled by it. We are living in days when God is separating the superficial from the sincere. My prayer is that this book helps strengthen you in your walk with God no matter the cost.

May the Lord give you a holy boldness, seasoned with humility, anchored in Scripture, and fueled by love.

Jack Hibbs,
Pastor, Calvary Chapel
President, Real Life Network

Introduction:
When the Church Stood Tall

"The church is looking for better methods;
God is looking for better men." ~ E.M. Bounds

IN 1988 GENERAL MOTORS MADE A CONCERTED effort to rebrand the Oldsmobile to boost sales. Their advertising campaign was "This is not your father's Oldsmobile." The campaign rebranded the Oldsmobile as more modern and youthful to appeal to younger customers. The previous Oldsmobiles were outdated and appealed to older people, the experts said. Ironically, the campaign had only short-term success because the Oldsmobile was eventually discontinued in 2004.

There has been a concerted effort in the last several decades to rebrand the church and make her more palatable to the younger generation. We are living in a day when compromise is called wisdom and cowardice is mistaken for kindness; where historic Christian doctrine is diluted, sin is rebranded, and the fear of man has replaced the fear of God. For things that matter the most, too many pulpits remain quiet and the people are left spiritually malnourished.

The church of the living God is resilient because it is the pillar and ground of the truth (1 Tim 3:15). This is not the first time God's church has faced internal decay or even cultural hostility. Yet it may be the first time so many have responded with retreat instead of resolve. Too many Christians and churches cave to social media pressure and bow before public opinion. They are afraid of being labeled judgmental and intolerant, and therefore being cancelled. Pews are full of people who are informed but not transformed; who are cowardly but not courageous.

This is why this book matters now. The church is in a time of moral compromise and spiritual retreat. The need is not for more programs or marketing strategies but for the church to stand tall and for God's truth to be proclaimed boldly. We need pastors to be strong like the prophets of old and their churches to stand on the uncompromising Word of God.

God's church has always been counter cultural. The church has flourished most when the fires of persecution burn hot. The second-century church father Tertullian is credited with saying "the blood of the martyrs is the seed of the church."[1] Fortunately, there is religious freedom in America where our lives are not at risk. What is needed today is the recovery of that same courage of the early church where people feared God more than man and counted everything but loss to win Christ.

There was a time when the church was feared by government tyrants, not because of her wealth or political connections but because she would not compromise on truth. The church today stands in stark contrast with the early church in that regard. The modern church is comfortable and affluent and does not want to "rock the boat." She courts the approval of social media and public opinion and avoids any hint of being labeled judgmental or divisive. The early church did not have the comforts of today but she did have what is lacking in today's church—courage rooted in biblical conviction.

Success was not measured by buildings and budgets but by commitment and sacrifice. Living a life of separation and holiness and declaring the truth of God was their passion and calling. Truly they wanted to please God more than men. This mindset caused them to be hated and persecuted throughout history. From the catacombs of Rome to the human bonfires of the English Reformation, from Baptist jails in Virginia to the underground churches in Communist China, the people of God stood out and stood courageously.

The modern church must reclaim her legacy of courage and truth. We stand on the shoulders of our forefathers who sacrificed so much for us. We should never forget their sacrifices and willingness to give their lives for the truth of the Gospel. At the Diet of Worms in AD 1521, Martin Luther courageously refused to recant and said, "Here I stand, I can do no other, so help me God." May that Holy Spirit courage be recovered today.

This book progresses in four parts, prayerfully building toward a revival of boldness as evidenced by our forefathers. The first part looks back in history to the early church martyrs, through the fires of the Reformation, to the bold pulpits of colonial America. The second part takes an honest and hard look in the mirror, revealing how the fear of man has crept into our preaching and theology and how that weakness is impacting the next generation. The third section is a rallying cry. It calls for courage in every aspect of the ministry of the church. Courage should not be a relic of the past but a requirement for the present. The last division delves into the fountainhead of courage. The source of our courage is God Himself supplying what is needed through spiritual disciplines and a daily walk with Christ.

We are standing at a crossroads in our time. The strong winds of compromise blow hard against the truth, and many seem content to drift. But God still looks for those who will stand, speak, and suffer, if necessary, for His name. The next chapter of church history is being written now, by us. May it be said of our generation that we stood firm, that we loved truth more than comfort, and that we followed Christ without retreat or apology.

May these pages awaken within you the same holy resolve that burned in those who came before us. I pray that the world might once again see a church alive with conviction, aflame with love, and anchored in courage until the Lord returns.

Section I:

A Heritage of Holy Boldness (The Historical Church)

1

Courage in the Early Church

"We must obey God rather than men." ~ Acts 5:29

THE STORY OF THE EARLY CHURCH IS ONE OF courage and boldness. The disciples fled in fear in the Garden of Gethsemane when Jesus was arrested by the lawless mob after the betrayal by Judas Iscariot. The disciples hid in fear during the cruel torture and bloody crucifixion of Jesus. After the death of Jesus, the disciples considered going back to their previous employment until they were instructed by their resurrected Lord to wait in Jerusalem until they were endued with power from on high (Luke 24:49).

However, on the day of Pentecost the one hundred and twenty men and women in the upper room, including the apostles, were all filled with the Holy Spirit and their lives were instantly transformed from fear to faith, from cowardliness to courage. When the multi-national crowd in Jerusalem heard these Spirit-filled believers speaking the Gospel in their native language, about three thousand committed their lives to Christ and were baptized (Acts 2:41). These transformed believers went everywhere declaring the Good News of salvation.

Not long after Pentecost, the Sanhedrin arrested Peter and John because they preached Jesus and the resurrection from the dead. When the Sanhedrin threatened them with punishment not to preach and teach any more about Jesus, they declared boldly, "We cannot but speak the things which we have seen and heard" (Acts 4:20). The church has now set a precedent to be obedient to God over obedience to man.

The apostles and early Christians did not retreat or stay silent in the face of opposition. They sought to obey God and boldly declare His Word. Their message declared the exclusivity of Jesus Christ for salvation which confronted sin and demanded repentance. That message, however, was not welcomed by the political and religious powers of the day. At every turn those leaders sought to crush the Christian movement and silence those who proclaimed the Gospel.

After Pentecost their preaching demonstrated courage that defied cultural pressure, religious opposition, and political threats. Their boldness was embedded in Holy

Spirit conviction and not worldly conceit. They were willing to pay whatever price was necessary, recalling the words of Jesus, "For whoever desires to save his life will lose it, but whoever loses his life for My sake and the gospel's will save it" (Mark 8:35).

The disciples were bold in their preaching. Standing before the religious leaders in Jerusalem and facing hostile crowds they declared, "God has made this Jesus, whom you crucified, both Lord and Christ" (Acts 2:36). This rhetoric cut to the heart and was not intended to cuddle the hearers but to convict them of their sin. These preachers were more concerned with being faithful than they were for being liked.

They were also bold in their praying. After Peter and John were arrested and mistreated by the authorities, they gathered the church and had a prayer meeting. Interestingly, they did not pray for safety but for more boldness. They did not want to retreat under the vicious threats. God answered their prayer by literally shaking the place where they were and they were filled with the Holy Spirit and continued to declare the Word of God with boldness (Acts 4:23–31). The fire of God was burning brightly in their lives which no man could extinguish.

Even in their suffering they were bold and unflinching. They were not reckless with their lives but rather they were resolved to be faithful to the Lord. Whenever they suffered for their faith, they would rejoice that they were counted worthy to suffer for Christ. They fully understood that suffering was a part of their ministry unlike many today. Jesus had taught them saying, "If the world hates you, you know that it hated Me before it hated you. If you were of the world, the world would love its own. Yet, because you are not of the world, but I chose you out of the world, therefore the world hates you" (John 15:18-19).

When they faced death, they did not cower but looked death boldly in the face. These faithful saints knew this world was not their home; there was something much better awaiting them. They did not water down the message; they did not try to win friends and influence people; they boldly proclaimed the truth even if it meant paying the ultimate price for that truth.

The deaths of the early Christians are a sobering and powerful testimony to their boldness and faith. Consider the following apostles and some martyrs of the early church and their witness to history. The apostle Peter was brutally crucified in Rome under Emperor Nero around AD 64. Tradition says that he felt unworthy to die in the same manner as his Lord, so he requested to be crucified upside down.

James, the son of Zebedee was beheaded in Jerusalem by order of King Herod Agrippa. He was the first of the apostles to be martyred but not the first Christian martyr;

that was Stephen who was stoned to death by hard-hearted Jews after he boldly preached Jesus to them.

John, the brother of James, was the only apostle to have died a natural death. Tertullian, a late second and third century Christian apologist, claims John was "plunged, unhurt, into boiling oil, and thence remitted to his island-exile [Patmos],"[2] where he wrote the book of Revelation. He was later freed and returned to Ephesus and died sometime after AD 98.

Andrew, Peter's brother, was crucified like his brother upside down but on an X-shaped cross in Patras, Greece around AD 60. Tradition says he preached to the people from the cross for two days before he died. The X-shaped cross called a saltire or St. Andrew's Cross became a symbol associated with his name.

Philip was crucified in Hierapolis (modern Turkey). Tradition says his death was an act of retaliation by the proconsul because Philip incurred the ire of the proconsul by leading his wife to the Christian faith.

Bartholomew met his death in India by being flayed alive and then beheaded. He received great opposition and fierce persecution at the hands of idolaters who viewed the Christian teaching as a direct threat to their religious practices and beliefs.

Matthew, the tax collector, spread the Gospel in Parthia and Ethiopia. He was speared to death in Ethiopia in the city of Nadabah in AD 60. The violent opposition he received was a testimony to his steadfast faith and effort to spread the Gospel.

Thomas was also called "the Twin" (John 11:16; 20:24), although scripture is silent as to the name of Thomas's twin. He earned the nickname "Doubting Thomas" because of his doubts and questions. He travelled by sea to the subcontinent of India and had some success but was met with great hostility. Syrian Christian tradition says Thomas was martyred in Mylapore in July AD 72.

James, the son of Alphaeus, is also called "James the Less" (Mark 15:40). Very little is known about James and there is little tradition known as well. Some say he may have taken the gospel to Persia (modern Iran) and was martyred there. Other tradition says he was thrown from the pinnacle of the temple then beaten to death with a club. His life is a picture of obscure service for our Lord.

Thaddaeus is referred to differently by the gospel writers. Matthew and Mark refer to him as "Thaddaeus" (Matt 10:3; Mark 3:18) while Luke refers to him as "Judas son of James" (Luke 6:16; Acts 1:13) and John calls him "Judas (not Iscariot)" (John 14:22). It is believed Thaddaeus took the gospel north and founded a church in Edessa, an area in modern Turkey. Tradition is mixed on how he died, either by being clubbed or crucified.

Simon was referred to as "the Zealot" possibly to

distinguish him from Simon Peter or to indicate his fervency for Jewish law or Jesus's teaching. He travelled to Persia (modern Iran) and shared the gospel. Tradition gives two ways in which he died. He was either sawn in half or crucified.[3]

The Apostle Paul was not one of the twelve but was a true apostle. He underwent a martyrs' death. After being imprisoned in Rome he was beheaded under Nero around AD 64–67.

Fast forward a few decades and the Romans were skilled in killing Christians. Polycarp, the aged bishop of Smyrna was arrested and brought to the arena. He was given the chance to save his life by reviling Christ and swearing to Caesar. Polycarp famously responded, "Eighty-six years have I served Him, and He has done me no wrong. How can I blaspheme my King who has saved me?"[4] When they threatened him with fire he told them fire would last a moment but the fire of God's judgment would last forever. When the fire was set, the flames did not consume him so they stabbed him to death.[5]

Tertullian, the fearless apologist from Carthage in North Africa, wrote against Roman paganism. He was the first to use the word "Trinity" when describing the Father, Son, and Holy Spirit as three distinct persons yet one essence. He famously said, "The blood of the martyrs is the seed of the church," emphasizing how persecution does not shrink the church but expands it under pressure.[6]

The early believers did not seek death but neither did they fear it. Suffering was seen as something to be avoided but also as a necessary calling underscoring what Jesus said: "If any man will come after Me, let him deny himself, take up his cross, and follow Me" (Matt 16:24). They lived with eternity in view because they knew that it was better to die in Christ than to live in compromise.

We live in a day when losing social status feels like persecution. Yet the early martyrs' deaths still speak great lessons to us, telling us that the gospel is more valuable than our comfort, truth is worth fighting for, and Jesus is worth living and even dying for. We inherited what the early martyrs died for. We should carry the torch they lit with their lives, boldly and faithfully.

2

The Reformation Fire

"Here I stand. I can do no other. So help me God. Amen."
~ Martin Luther

THE EARLY CHURCH BELIEVERS GAVE US A picture of their courage and boldness in the face of severe pagan brutality. Yet they did not flinch but "loved not their lives unto death." The Reformation gave us a portrait of unwavering conviction against religious corruption. The early believers stood against wicked emperors, false gods, and hungry lions in the colosseum. The Reformers stood against popes, councils, and an ecclesial structure that had buried the gospel of Christ beneath layers of man-made tradition.

The courage of the Reformers was no less perilous than the early believers. They were not subjected to the brutality of the lions but to the depraved callousness of a religious human heart. The early believers' "crime" was to say "Jesus is Lord" instead of "Caesar is Lord." The Reformers "crime" was to declare the Word of God above the word of Rome. The Reformers' intent was not to destroy the church but to purge it of corruption. Those noble men stood on the solid rock of *sola scriptura*, Scripture alone, not on the encyclicals of the Pope. Because of their stand on the Bible alone they were branded as heretics, hunted like criminals, imprisoned, and many were burned alive.

John Wycliffe, a 14th century Oxford theologian, is referred to as the "Morning Star of the Reformation." He believed that Holy Scripture, not church tradition, was the ultimate authority for faith and life. In his day the Latin Vulgate was the main Bible available and they were kept in churches. A common person could not read it because it was in Latin and the people had to rely on the local priest to tell them what the Bible said. Believing that the Bible should be in the language of the common people, Wycliffe translated the Scriptures from Latin into English in AD 1380. All copies were handwritten because the printing press had not been invented.

Wycliffe's followers, known as the Lollards, carried both the Scriptures and his teachings far beyond England's borders, even reaching as far as Bohemia (modern day Czechoslovakia). There, a Roman Catholic priest named Jan Hus encountered Wycliffe's writings, which deepened his growing concern over the corruption and errors within the Church. For their steadfast devotion to biblical truth, both the Lollards and Hus were branded as heretics and suffered violent persecution at the hands of the established Church. Yet their courage and conviction helped keep the light of God's Word burning in a dark and fearful age.

William Tyndale, an early 16th-century English Reformer, was deeply influenced by the teachings of John Wycliffe. Like Wycliffe, he was convinced that the Word of God—not the word of Rome—was what the people truly needed. Tyndale longed for every plowboy in England to have access to the Scriptures in his own language. With this conviction burning in his heart, he produced the first printed English New Testament, opening the pages of God's Word to common men and women for the first time.

But such holy boldness came at a high cost. Branded a heretic by the established Church, Tyndale was hunted, betrayed, and eventually captured. On October 6, AD 1536, he was executed by strangulation and then burned at the stake. As the flames rose, his final prayer rang out through history: "Lord, open the king of England's eyes."[7] In time, that prayer was answered, as the English Bible was authorized and the gospel spread freely across the land.

The invention of the printing press enabled the Bible to be printed into the language of the people. This action supercharged the Reformation because the more people read the Bible for themselves the more their eyes were open to see the sharp divergence between what the Bible taught and what the Roman Catholic Church practiced. The proliferation of the Bible created great tension between the established church and the people who read it.

The institutional church of Rome over the course of time had strayed dangerously far from the doctrinal teachings of Holy Scripture. Instead of standing under the authority of the Word of God the Roman Church claimed she had equal authority through tradition, papal decrees, and church councils. Doctrines such as purgatory, indulgences, transubstantiation, and the veneration of saints had no biblical basis but were upheld as binding truths.

The biblical basis of salvation had been lost in the maze of tradition and false teaching. Through the sale of indulgences sinners were promised reduced time in purgatory, for themselves or loved ones, in exchange for financial gifts to the Church. These monies were to be used to build St. Peter's Basilica in Rome. This scheme was created by Johann Tetzel and approved by the Pope. The people of Europe under the Roman Catholic Church were kept in great ignorance. Tetzel preyed on their superstitious fears to convince people their departed dead were burning in flames in purgatory and they should pay money to free them from their torment. Tetzel is credited with the jingle, "As soon as the coin in the coffer rings, the soul from purgatory springs."[8]

The German Augustinian monk named Martin Luther had desperately tried to find peace with God by human works. After all his extraordinary attempts failed the Holy Spirit shattered his spiritual darkness as he was studying the book of Romans. A verse in Rom 1:17, "The just shall live by faith," pierced his soul like a bolt of lightning. Luther's eyes were opened to the truth that righteousness before God is not earned through penance, prayers, or payments but by faith alone in Jesus Christ. This was the spark that ignited Reformation fires that spread throughout Europe.

Reacting against Tetzel and his indulgences Luther posted his now famous "95 Theses" on the Wittenberg Castle Church door on October 31, AD 1517. The first points of Luther's 95 "Theses" challenged the sale of indulgences and called the Church back to biblical repentance and the Word of God. Luther's actions created quite a stir in Germany and quickly the news spread to Rome.

Luther's writings were decreed to be heretical by Pope Leo X in July AD 1520. At the Diet of Worms in AD 1521, Luther was ordered to recant his writings. After a night of prayer he responded to the council, "Unless I am convicted by Scripture and plain reason—I do not accept the authority of popes and councils, for they have contradicted each other—my conscience is captive to the Word of God. I cannot and I will not recant anything, for to go against conscience is neither right nor safe. God help me. Amen."[9] Refusing to do so Luther was excommunicated from the Catholic Church in January AD 1521 and his writings were to be burned.[10]

While Luther and other Magisterial Reformers like Calvin and Zwingli challenged the theological errors of Rome, many Anabaptists believed the Reformation did not go far enough. These "re-baptizers" (*Wiedertäufer*), as they were called,[11] insisted that the Church must not only be reformed in doctrine but restored in practice. The Reformers wanted to reform the Church but the Anabaptists wanted to return to the practice of the New Testament. These Anabaptists were not only critical of the Roman Catholic Church but they were also critical of the Reformed Church. Although the Reformed Church had made great progress in returning to some biblical doctrines, the Reformers did not go far enough for the Anabaptists. The Anabaptists found themselves in a quandary being persecuted by both the Catholics and the Reformers.

The Reformers made great strides in clarifying five great pillars of biblical truth now known as the Five Solas: *Sola Scriptura*—Scripture Alone; *Sola Fide*—Faith Alone;

Sola Gratia—Grace Alone; *Solus Christus*—Christ Alone; and *Soli Deo Gloria*—To the Glory of God Alone. These were the battle cries of the Reformers but the Anabaptists also agreed with these five truths.

The contentions between the Reformers and the Anabaptists centered around baptism, the candidate and mode, and the separation of church from the state.[12] At the heart of Anabaptist theology was the conviction that only those who personally professed faith in Christ should be baptized. This was a direct rejection of infant baptism which was universally practiced by Roman Catholics and most Reformers.

This belief was not simply unpopular; it was illegal since the church and state were wed. To reject infant baptism was to be branded a heretic by the church and an enemy of the state. Felix Manz, a Swiss Anabaptist and a student under the Reformer Ulrich Zwingli, was among the first to be martyred for preaching believer's baptism. On January 5, AD 1527, the Zurich city council (with Zwingli's consent) sentenced Manz to death by drowning. His mother and brother stood on the shore cheering him on in the faith as he sank beneath the water.

The Anabaptist also taught that the church should be free from the control of the civil government. This idea was foreign to the Catholics and Reformers at this time where the church and state were intertwined. To the Reformers, the magistrate had a duty to uphold what they considered correct doctrine. The Anabaptists, however, insisted that no government had the right to compel faith or interfere with the worship of Christ. This conviction did not come from rebellion but from Scripture. They believed Christ was the head of the church, not the Pope or the state.

The courage of the Anabaptists in continental Europe did not die with the martyrs drowned in the Limmant River or in the burned ashes in the squares of Zurich and Vienna. Their blood watered seeds that would eventually sprout across the English Channel.

The same convictions that drove the Anabaptists, Scripture over tradition, Christ over kings, and a church of true believers, began to stir in the hearts of the English Separatists. Many of these Separatists would soon embrace the very principles that had marked the Anabaptists as heretics. From this soil, the English Baptists would emerge as heirs of the same courageous spirit that had once defied both pope and magistrate on the continent.

In the early AD 1600's Thomas Helwys, an English lawyer and theologian, allied with the Puritans and the Separatists because these groups were critical of the Church of England. When the dissenting congregation came under persecution by King James I as head of the Church of England, Helwys believed the Church of England was beyond repair and separated, but many of the Puritans thought otherwise and stayed. Ultimately Helwys broke away from the Separatists as he rejected infant baptism. He also separated from the Puritans over religious freedom since they held to the divine right of kings. This doctrine asserted that kings derived their authority from God and therefore could not be held accountable for their actions by any earthly authority. Helwys is noted for forming the first Baptist church on English soil.

Thomas Helwys boldly wrote to King James I in AD 1612: "although a king, was but a mortal man and as a mortal man, though a king, had no authority whatever over the consciences of his subjects."[13] For his boldness Helwys was imprisoned in Newgate Prison where he died in AD 1616.

The persecution of the courageous Reformers now taking on the Baptist moniker did not end at the shores of the Atlantic. When Baptists eventually crossed the ocean to the New World they hoped for a land of liberty where their freedom of conscience could be respected and the gospel could flourish. But old habits die hard. The same convictions that made them outcasts and martyrs in Europe and England (which were believer's baptism, the independence of the local church, and the separation of church and state) soon made them targets in the American colonies.

They had escaped the kings and councils of Europe

and England, yet persecution followed them across the sea. In the New World, Puritan magistrates and the established churches of colonies like Massachusetts and Virginia took up the same tools of oppression, stocks, fines, whippings, and imprisonment for any who dared to defy the state-sanctioned faith. America promised a new beginning for these courageous believers, but the struggle for soul freedom was far from over; in truth, it had only begun.

3

Courage on the American Soil

"Resistance to tyranny become the Christian and social duty of each individual." ~ John Witherspoon

THE JOURNEY FROM ENGLAND TO AMERICA WAS not just a voyage across the Atlantic, it was a continuation of the same spiritual battles that had been waged in Europe and England. The English Separatists and Baptists came to the new land seeking opportunities where Christ's church could be free from the chains of the state and people could worship God according to the dictates of their conscience. But when they arrived, they found that Massachusetts and Virginia were just new landscapes occupied by old enemies, state established churches, enforced uniformity, and the persecution of conscience. Their aspirations of religious freedom were quickly shattered but that setback did not diminish their courage but rather strengthened their resolve for a new life in a new land.

The story of religious freedom in America was not written in lofty palaces but was forged from being banished from the community, thrown into crude prison cells, flogged until having bloody backs at the public whipping post, and from an unshakable biblical conviction in the Word of God over tradition. The courageous men who carried the torch from England to the colonies were not astute politicians or military leaders but were pastors and preachers, ordinary believers with extraordinary convictions.

Roger Williams was one of many examples of courage on American soil. He was ordained in the Church of England and married a Puritan pastor's daughter. It was not long until his separatist views and strong moral convictions led him to migrate to the New World. He arrived in Massachusetts Bay Colony in AD 1631 seeking refuge from persecution in England. His argument for the separation of church and state which was a revolutionary idea at the time, quickly brought him into conflict with Puritan leaders. In AD 1635 he was banished from the colony for advocating "liberty of soul" and he was forced to flee into the wilderness during the harsh winter months.

The Narragansett Indians took him in and saved his life. The next year he purchased land from the tribe and founded Providence Plantations on the principle "soul freedom," believing that worship should not be forced on the individual. The settlement became a haven for people seeking religious toleration and freedom from persecution.

Williams's settlement became the first in the New World to offer full religious freedom, even for those of other faiths. He argued that it is God's will "that ... a permission of the most paganish, Jewish, Turkish, or antichristian consciences and worships be granted to all men in all nations and countries."[14] Williams helped found the first Baptist church in the New World. He later returned to England to obtain a charter for Rhode Island and served as the colony's first president.

Another courageous New Englander who was willing to speak up was John Clarke. Clarke was more than just a minister; he was also a trained physician. Not long after Clarke emigrated to Boston from England, he joined Roger Williams in Rhode Island because of the religious restrictions in Massachusetts Bay. He became the co-founder of Newport, Rhode Island, and organized the First Baptist Church of Newport, one of the earliest Baptist congregations in America.[15]

John Clarke was also the chief architect of Rhode Island's religious liberty laws and played a critical role in securing the 1663 Rhode Island Charter which guaranteed that no person would be "molested, punished, disquieted, or called in question for any differences in opinion in matters of religion."[16]

The story of Obadiah Holmes[17] and his courage and convictions in the face of severe persecution by the Puritans in Massachusetts began to open hearts to the idea of freedom of worship. Reverend Obadiah Holmes came to Salem, Massachusetts from England around AD 1639. He was a Congregationalist for many years and became a Baptist in Newport, Rhode Island, being influenced by John Clarke. In July AD 1651 he visited William Witter, a Baptist who lived in Lynn, Massachusetts, about twelve miles from Boston. Accompanying Holmes was John Clark and John Crandall.

While there they attended a small religious service in Witter's house. In the midst of the service two constables burst in and arrested them and took them to jail in Boston. Their worship in Witter's house was deemed illegal because it was outside the state church's authority. The three men were charged with conducting an unauthorized religious service and were given a fine; Obadiah Holmes thirty pounds, John Clarke twenty pounds, and John Crandall five pounds. This was a substantial amount in that day. If they did not pay the fine, they were to be publicly whipped. Friends of Clarke and Crandall paid their fines but Holmes refused to let them on the principle that to pay would be to admit guilt in obeying Christ's command to worship.

On September 5, AD 1651, Holmes was led to the whipping post in Boston Commons. Stripped to the waist, he received thirty lashes with a three-corded whip wielded so fiercely that witnesses later said the executioner "wore out his strength before he had finished."[18] The flogging left him so wounded he could only rest on his elbows and knees for weeks afterward.

Yet Holmes's courage became a rallying point for dissenters and Baptists who stood for freedom of worship in the colonies. The persecution of the state church by the Puritans backfired and the concept of "soul freedom" spread rapidly. The seeds of religious liberty and biblical truth were planted in the soil of suffering. The persecution of Obadiah Holmes had stirred in the heart of Henry Dunster, President of Cambridge College (now Harvard University), such that he refused to have his infant son baptized and was forced to resign his presidency.[19]

Religious liberty was being fought for in the courtrooms and town squares but it was also being advanced in pulpits that refused to soften the gospel. The 18th century brought a spiritual earthquake to the colonies in the first Great Awakening. This movement of God was led by men of God whose courage was in preaching the truth with piercing clarity.

The Great Awakening seemed to have been ignited by the preaching of Jonathan Edwards, a Congregational pastor in Northampton, Massachusetts. Edwards was a man with great theological depth and confronted the spiritual apathy of his day. His sermon, *Sinners in the Hands of an Angry God*, painted the torments of a soul apart from Christ and eternity with such vivid realism that the hearers reportedly clung to their pews in fear of slipping into hell.

Edwards refused to dilute biblical truth to preserve his popularity even when it cost him his pulpit. His insistence on standing for biblical truth led to his dismissal in AD 1750. He later became the president of the College of New Jersey (which would become Princeton University) in AD 1758.

Evangelist George Whitefield, indisputably the most popular preacher in America, had a very powerful impact on the culture in the colonies and his preaching helped to fuel the fire of the Great Awakening. Whitefield detested lukewarm Christianity and refused to soft-peddle his preaching. He made every effort to shake churchgoers out of their apathy.

Whitefield, an Anglican evangelist from England, preached to crowds that sometimes exceeded 20,000 people in the open air. Most churches could not accommodate the crowds and other churches would not allow Whitefield in their pulpits. He often preached in meadows at the edge of cities. These outdoor meetings were considered nothing less than sacrilege to the proper church folk of his day. Not deterred by the resistance of the religious establishment, Whitefield would preach to any group that would listen. He had an unshakable resolve to proclaim the necessity of the new birth in Christ. His fearless preaching united the colonies in revival and stirred hearts toward liberty. He constantly reminded the people that, whether it be the state or the church, no earthly power had the right to enslave the soul.

The battle for soul liberty and freedom from tyranny in the colonies was not confined to New England. In colonial Virginia, the struggle took on a different form but sprang from the same root. The established state church determined to suppress any preaching outside her control. Here, the Anglican establishment wielded the power of law to silence dissent. However, those courageous dissenters would meet the challenge with the same courage, conviction, and determination that had marked their brethren in Massachusetts.

In Virginia, the Anglican establishment required all preachers to be licensed by the state church. James Ireland rejected religion in his younger years in Scotland. After he came to America, he found faith in Christ and began sharing the message of salvation everywhere he went. This led the state church to report him and he was jailed for preaching without permission. Crowds would gather around the prison window to hear him preach. While in prison his enemies tried to poison him and even to suffocate him by burning brimstone at the door and window of his cell, but he was not deterred. Upon his release he resumed preaching and inspired younger ministers to stand courageously for truth and against religious oppression. Over time his persecutions permanently destroyed his health and he died on May 5, 1806.[20]

The courage of James Ireland in his pulpit and in prison was a testimony of endurance. He stood firm when others were silenced by threats and intimidation. However, the struggle for religious freedom did not end at the jailhouse door. What these preachers won with their wounds, others had to secure with their words. The fight was transitioning from the whipping post to the halls of government. In this new arena no one carried the banner of truth and liberty higher than John Leland, the statesman of soul freedom.

John Leland, a preacher with Baptist convictions, had uncommon fire and wit with astute political insight. Leland moved to Virginia from Massachusetts and became a neighbor of James Madison and Thomas Jefferson. He spent years ministering in Virginia where Baptists were still harassed by Anglican authorities. Leland often mocked the pride of politicians and the pomp of churchmen. Yet beneath his audacious humor was an unshakable conviction that the gospel needs no state sponsor and the conscience of man should bow only to Christ.

Leland returned to Cheshire, Massachusetts and a few years later Thomas Jefferson was elected President by the House of Representatives on the thirty-sixth ballot. Leland believed America had a president that understood the common man. To celebrate this event "all the milk from nine hundred local, loyal Republican cows was collected and brought into Cheshire, where the population gathered to sing hymns, socialize, and make cheese. The product of this effort was a mammoth cheese wheel four feet, four and one-half inches in diameter, fifteen inches thick, and weighing 1,235 pounds."[21]

Leland was elected to take the cheese to the President in Washington, D.C. and preached to the crowds along the way. When the cheese was presented to the President, Leland was to assure him "that no Federalist cows had contributed milk to the cheese, only Democratic-Republican cows."[22] The cheese was a symbol of gratitude for Jefferson's stand against an established church and his defense of liberty of conscience.

The road to religious freedom in America, which has become a beacon for the world, was a road paved with great courage and conviction. These brave soldiers of Christ were not seeking comfort, prestige, or popularity. They were living for the glory of Christ and the truth of the gospel even when that meant banishment, beatings, and prison bars. Their courage gave us inspiring stories and the framework of freedom that still protects us today.

Freedom, however, is never self-sustaining. Every generation must decide whether liberty is worth the price. Our forefathers and mothers handed us a heritage of conscience unchained, a gospel unbound, and a church free to follow Christ alone. The question now comes to us: will we honor their sacrifice by living with the same convictions and courage?

For if we in our comfort and convenience let fear silence us then we will squander what they secured at such a cost. But if we, in our day, live as they did, boldly, faithfully, unashamedly, then God's truth will blaze forth and the Church of Jesus Christ will continue to be a witness to the world and a conviction to the corrupt culture of the day.

This kind of courage is not born out of ease or nurtured by societal applause but is forged in the furnace of biblical conviction. We must ask what does courage look like in our time? How can believers today recover that same fire that burned in the hearts of our forefathers? They stood firm, spoke truth, and suffered gladly for our Lord, and so must we.

For if the church of the first century faced lions, the church of the twenty-first century faces lies. Both require courage. Both demand faith. The world may have changed but the gospel has not, and neither has the call to declare it without fear.

Section II:

The Decline of Courage
(The Contemporary Crisis)

4

The Cowardice of Compromise

"A man who won't stand for something will fall for anything."
~ Alexander Hamilton

THE STORY OF THE CHURCH IS NOT MERELY ONE of triumph but also of tragedy. For every age where great courage has been displayed there comes a season of compromise. If Christians in previous generations shed their blood to propagate and preserve the truth many in our time have shed only their convictions. The battlefield has not disappeared; it has only shifted. Early in the spiritual conflict the enemies were lions in the arena, tortures on the rack, and the flames of being burned at the stake. Today the spiritual warfronts are creature comforts, cultural approval, and the ever-present temptation to water down the truth to make it palatable to others to avoid offense.

Alexander Hamilton's piercing warning two-hundred and fifty years ago still rings true today: *A man who won't stand for something will fall for anything.* In too many pulpits and pews across our great land silence has replaced boldness, softness has been substituted for strength, and the gospel of Christ and truth of Holy Scripture has been reduced to fit the fashions of this age. Where once the church of Jesus Christ shaped culture, now the culture shapes much of the church. This is the cowardice of compromise and its fruit is evident all around in shallow preaching, fragile faith, and a generation that scarcely knows the Bible.

Psalm 11:3 asks the haunting and penetrating question: *If the foundations be destroyed, what can the righteous do?* We are living in a day and hour when the foundations of what our forefathers lived and died for are being slowly chipped away. Those virtues of absolute truth, biblical holiness, moral clarity, and family values are eroding before our very eyes. There are few courageous voices crying out in the wilderness and standing against the cultural current calling us back to those values which made us great and caused us to prosper in God's blessings.

The decline of courageous preachers declaring *thus says the Lord* has left us with churches that struggle to discern right from wrong and quickly surrender to the world under cultural pressure. It is time for God's people to repent and return to the Lord for the strength of conviction and the truth that once turned the world upside down.

Every generation of believers has been faced with the temptation to compromise the truth in order to gain popularity and receive the world's approval. Our Lord warned of this when He said, "Woe to you, when all men shall speak well of you, For so did their fathers to the false prophets" (Luke 6:26). Yet much of western Christianity and the modern church has fallen into that very snare. Where sin was once clearly denounced it is now rationalized and excused. God's truth once thundered from pulpits but now it whispers as if those declaring it are ashamed.

The church in the west has been severely diminished because she has been silent in the face of sin and at times even promoted sin. She has capitulated to the culture to appear more loving and understanding only to discover the Lord has written "Icabod" over her door. Too many churches have lost the gospel and have become worldly and powerless.

One of the greatest threats to the modern church is her willingness to conform its theology and morality to the surrounding culture. What begins as "relevance" often ends up as compromise. Throughout history God's people have been called to be a holy people and the church to be a witness to the world (1 Pet 2:9–12). Yet time and again the church has chosen to blend into the world rather than stand out.

For generations, evangelicals in America drew a clear line when it came to alcohol and entertainment. A person claiming to be a teetotaler was not just a social preference but a testimony to holiness and separation. Yet in recent years, many churches have embraced the very culture they once warned against, complete with "theology on tap" events and open discussions of explicit entertainment, defended under the guise of cultural engagement. As one writer observed, evangelicals have exchanged moral clarity for cultural acceptance, blurring the lines between holiness and worldliness.[23]

In order to boost dwindling numbers in church attendance and attract new people, novel approaches have been advanced. Some churches have experimented by uniting hymns with beer.[24] The sharpness of previous generations' moral distinctiveness has been dulled by the present cultural accommodation.

Perhaps one of the clearest examples of cultural accommodation in modern church history can be seen in the Southern Baptist Convention's (SBC) response to *Roe v. Wade*. When the U.S. Supreme Court handed down its decision in AD 1973 legalizing abortion nationwide, the SBC did not immediately stand as the bold defender of unborn life that many imagine today. Instead, the denomination initially mirrored the broader culture's acceptance of abortion as a matter of personal choice and medical freedom.

In fact, in AD 1971, two years before *Roe v. Wade*, the SBC passed a resolution calling for the legalization of abortion under broad circumstances, including "carefully ascertained cases of rape, incest, clear evidence of severe fetal deformity, and carefully ascertained evidence of the likelihood of damage to the emotional, mental, and physical health of the mother."[25] After *Roe v. Wade* was decided, the Convention in AD 1974[26] and again in AD 1976[27] passed resolutions that essentially accepted the Supreme Court's ruling, framing abortion as a complicated issue where individual conscience and government policy should prevail rather than Scripture's clear witness to the sanctity of life.

This accommodation was nothing less than capitulation to the spirit of the age. While culture celebrated "women's liberation" and personal autonomy, the SBC (fearful of appearing out of step) chose silence and softness where courage and conviction were demanded. Instead of proclaiming the biblical truth that life begins in the womb[28] the largest Protestant denomination in America bowed to cultural winds.

Yet by the late 1970s and early 1980s with the rise of

the pro-life movement and the Conservative Resurgence within the SBC, there was a dramatic reversal. Leaders like Paige Patterson and Adrian Rogers helped bring the denomination back to her biblical roots, calling abortion what it is, the taking of innocent human life. In AD 1980 the SBC adopted a resolution that reaffirmed the biblical view of the "sacredness and dignity of all human life born and unborn"[29] making a clear renunciation of its earlier accommodation. From that point forward, the Convention became one of the loudest denominational voices for the pro-life cause, repeatedly urging the overturning of *Roe v. Wade* and supporting legislation to protect the unborn.

The lesson is sobering. The SBC's initial support of *Roe v. Wade* stands as a stark reminder of what happens when God's people allow culture, not Scripture, to set its moral compass. But the reversal of the SBC also demonstrates that God's people, when convicted by His Word, can return to courage and clarity. Accommodation may win applause in the short term, but only conviction wins God's approval in eternity.

Another example of where the culture has infiltrated the church (leading to moral compromise) is in the Revoice Movement. On the surface this movement appeared to be a faithful attempt to bridge the gap between compassion for those experiencing same-sex attraction and the conviction of what the Bible says about homosexuality. However, the language and practice embraced by Revoice has created significant concerns that reveal deep moral and theological compromise.

The acceptance of LGBTQ identity language within the life of a believer is an oxymoron. Referring to oneself as a "gay Christian" or "LGBTQ Christian" is inconsistent with biblical language. This language embeds sinful desires into the believer's identity. Instead of defining themselves first and foremost as new creatures in Christ[30] they are attempting to normalize sin as a permanent category of selfhood. Instead of encouraging believers to seek God's power to change desires and live in holiness, Revoice frames same-sex attraction as a life-long, unchangeable condition. This undercuts the gospel's call to sanctification, thus making biblical holiness unattainable.

Perhaps the gravest compromise is that Revoice has shifted the church's message from one of prophetic clarity to therapeutic accommodation. Affirming one's identity that is rooted in sin and celebrates aspects of a corrupt culture contradicts the clarion gospel call to die to self and walk in holiness. This is the equivalence of the trumpet making an uncertain sound which leads to chaos and confusion.

The church of Jesus Christ was never meant to be a mirror of the world but a light to it. Cultural accommodation has weakened the modern church and left her witness tarnished. When truth is trimmed to fit the fashions of the age courage withers, conviction weakens, and compromise reigns. The result is a gospel that no longer confronts sin, a pulpit that no longer thunders with conviction, and a people who no longer stand distinct from the world they are called to reach.

When the church yields to cultural pressure it forfeits its power and prophetic voice. The applause of men is fleeting; the judgment of God is eternal. The more a church seeks to be relevant in society the more irrelevant she becomes. The pursuit of acceptance has proven to be costly, leaving her message diluted and her witness dimmed. Will the church stand boldly for truth or will she fall for the lies of the age? Before healing can come honesty must prevail. Only when the problem is clearly addressed can the church rediscover her courage and renew her strength.

5

Diagnosing the Modern Church

"If the foundations be destroyed,
what can the righteous do?" ~ Psalm 11:3

EVERY GENERATION OF BELIEVERS MUST FACE the sobering question: What is the true condition of Christ's church in our time? It is easy to be impressed by what the eye can see, the large building, the active programs, and the impressive budgets. Yet God does not measure His church by outward strength but by inward faithfulness. The modern church in the West stands at a critical crossroads. Outwardly, she appears strong, but inwardly she is fragile. Her roots are withering and her backbone has weakened because she has too often drifted from the solid ground of truth she once held so dearly. The psalmist's haunting words echo over our generation: "If the foundations are destroyed, what can the righteous do?" (Ps

11:3). The bedrock of biblical conviction, doctrinal depth, and moral clarity that once defined the church is now eroding before our very eyes. Though she still looks outwardly healthy she is, in many ways, spiritually ill and is suffering from a heart condition that only repentance and truth can heal.

The tragedy of our age is that the church has mistaken activity for vitality. She is busy with many things but not necessarily fruitful. The machinery of ministry turns faster than ever, yet there is very little evidence of lasting transformation. Many churches are more concerned with maintaining attendance than with proclaiming repentance. The message of the cross has been modified, the weight of sin has been minimized, and the holiness of God has been neglected, all to be culturally relevant and to find acceptance. The church has become skilled in marketing but weak in moral clarity. As a result, she is no longer shaping the culture; she is being shaped by it.

Historically, the strength of the church was never found in numbers, wealth, or influence, but in her conviction and courage. When she stood firmly upon the Word of God, she stood tall before the world. But when she began to seek the world's approval by wavering on the truth, she lost her spiritual authority. The early believers turned the world upside down because they refused to seek her approval. Today, however, many churches bend to the winds of public opinion, adjusting the message to fit the mood of the age. In doing so, they have traded their prophetic voice for cultural applause.

The crisis is not merely theological; it is spiritual. We are witnessing a slow erosion of reverence, a loss of the fear of God that once anchored the people of faith. Entertainment has replaced worship. Feelings have replaced truth. The result is a generation of professing believers who know the language of faith but not the life of faith. The church has become broad in appearance but shallow in depth, loud in expression but quiet in conviction.

If the disease of compromise is to be cured, the church must recover what she has lost. She must return to her foundations; the authority of Scripture, the preaching of the gospel, and the pursuit of holiness. Only then can her strength be renewed and her witness be restored.

Throughout America, church surveys have revealed a steady, but significant, decline of attendance. This decline is easily observed but what is more difficult to see is the weakening of conviction. The American Bible Society State of the Bible report in 2022 reported an "unprecedented drop in the percentage of Bible users in the United States"[31] dropping from 50% to 39%, the lowest one year drop in a decade. George Barna, Senior Research Fellow at the Center for Biblical Worldview Family Research Council, found that "43% of adult churchgoers claim to have a biblical worldview. However, extensive testing through the American Worldview Inventory indicates that just 6% of the adult population actually has one."[32] These statistics are not merely numbers; they reveal symptoms of a spiritual sickness that has affected the churches.

The church has been infected with doctrinal compromise and the loss of courageous pastors boldly declaring the Word of God. Where pulpits once thundered with the authority of God's Word it now too often whispers smooth high sounding religious platitudes designed more to placate the culture than to confront sin. David Wells, Distinguished Senior Research Professor at Gordon-Conwell Theological Seminary, has described this as "the weightlessness of God"[33] in modern evangelicalism. God has become a small thought, a peripheral concern, while we humans want to dominate the stage. Preaching has been reduced from "thus says the Lord" to motivational talks leaving the church ill-prepared to "contend earnestly for the faith which was once for all delivered to the saints" (Jude 3) and to stand against the pressures of a hostile world.

There must be an honest appraisal of the church's weakened condition if she is to recover to her historical biblical positions. When a sick person goes to a doctor the physician must first examine the patient and run tests to identify the problem before prescribing treatment. Even so this chapter will endeavor to diagnose some of those causes that have contributed to the church's decline and loss of influence in society. There must be appropriate actions following the analysis to return the church back to her mission. Only then can we call the church back to health through repentance and renewal rooted in the Word of God.

One of the most evident symptoms of the modern church's sickness is the poverty of the pulpit. Where once preachers labored to preach the Bible and expound the whole counsel of God (Acts 20:27), many pulpits today serve up amusing stories and feel-good lessons. The gospel of Christ where repentance and faith were once declared has often been replaced with motivational speeches and "how-to" talks that appeal to felt needs rather than confront sin.

The spirit of our age has become far more therapeutic than theological, and sadly, much of modern preaching has followed that trend. Secular psychology has been dressed in religious language and presented as gospel truth. Instead of calling sinners to repentance and faith in Christ for the forgiveness of sins, many sermons now aim merely to calm anxieties, boost self-esteem, and offer practical advice for living a happier life. In doing so, the pulpit has traded conviction for comfort and truth for therapy.

The therapeutic turn in Western culture has profoundly reshaped how people view themselves and what they expect from religion. Philip Rieff, in his seminal work *The Triumph of the Therapeutic*, argued that modern man has shifted from a culture of authority and morality to one of therapy, where the highest good is personal happiness and emotional well-being.[34] In this postmodern climate, sin is no longer a moral rebellion against a holy God but a psychological obstacle to self-fulfillment. This shift has proven irresistible to many churches whose primary intent is growth.

Sociologists Christian Smith and Melinda Lundquist Denton gave this phenomenon a memorable label in their study of American youth religion as "Moralistic Therapeutic Deism." According to their research, the de facto religion of many churchgoers boils down to five principles: (1) God exists and created the world; (2) He wants people to be good and nice; (3) the central goal of life is to be happy and feel good about oneself; (4) God is only needed to solve problems; and (5) good people go to heaven when they die. This is a system in which God exists to help us feel better and achieve our personal goals but without making demands of holiness or calling us to obedience to God.[35]

David Wells captured the church's capitulation to this therapeutic culture with poignant clarity. In his piercing book *No Place for Truth*, he wrote, "Theology becomes therapy, and all the telltale symptoms of the therapeutic model of faith begin to surface. The biblical interest in righteousness is replaced by a search for happiness, holiness by wholeness, truth by feeling, ethics by feeling good about one's self ... All that remains is the self."[36] The therapeutic culture is not neutral, it is corrosive. By catering to imagined felt needs rather than addressing real spiritual needs it redefines the role of God from sovereign Lord to cosmic therapist.

The fruit of this shift is very destructive. When sermons are designed primarily to uplift rather than to convict, churches may grow numerically but will shrink spiritually. The gospel is changed and becomes less about the glory of Christ and more about the well-being of man. Historian Carl Trueman noted in *The Rise and Triumph of the Modern Self* that the modern West has embraced what Charles Taylor refers to as "expressive individualism,"[37] the idea that true identity is found in looking within and affirming one's inner feelings. Preaching of this sort offers God as the guarantor of our personal authenticity rather than the One who commands us to deny ourselves, take up our cross, and follow Christ (Luke 9:23).

This therapeutic emphasis has transformed drastically the content and tone of preaching. Historically, preaching aimed to confront men and women with their sin calling forth repentance and the necessity of salvation through Christ alone and his atoning work on Calvary's cross. Jonathan Edwards, in the First Great Awakening, could preach *Sinners in the Hands of an Angry God* because he believed eternity hung in the balance for every hearer. In contrast, modern preaching often seeks to encourage hearers to "be their best selves."

This is not merely a stylistic change but a theological one where the cross becomes less about satisfying divine justice and more about demonstrating God's acceptance of us as we are. The danger of this shift is obvious. Preaching is emptied of the seriousness and sinfulness of sin and God's gracious offer of forgiveness of sins is abandoned. Congregations are left to be superficially comforted but tragically deceived and spiritually impoverished. Martyn Lloyd-Jones discerned this trend decades ago. He warned, "Any study of church history and any analysis of the troubles of the Church today and at all times will show that the ultimate cause of trouble is a departure from the authority of the Scriptures."[38]

Again, George Barna through his research shed light on the problem. American churches have failed to preach about sin, which Barna says has been destructive to the church. His 2019 research that "analyzed sermon content across the nation determined that just 3% of all sermons preached even mentioned sin. That's a devastating bodyblow to the Church world."[39] Barna went on to say, "For an overwhelming majority of Christian churches to suppress the reality of sin, its consequences, and its solutions from the people those churches serve is a travesty."[40]

Congregations that are constantly fed with milk and not solid food (1 Cor 3:1-3) cannot be expected to withstand the strong winds of cultural hostility. Jesus warned that those with no root would "endure only for a time. Afterward, when tribulation or persecution arises for the word's sake, immediately they stumble" (Mark 4:17). The fragility of modern faith was made plain during the COVID-19 pandemic, when churches across America shut down, only to see that when they reopened attendance collapsed. Pew Research found that by late 2020, nearly a third of those who had been regular churchgoers prior to the pandemic had stopped attending altogether, either in person or online.[41]

The secular culture has shaped the content of preaching but it has also altered its very function. Historically preaching was marked by a deep, exposition of Scripture. The Puritans, for instance, were known for their "plain preaching" of the Word of God where the goal was to unfold the text in its fullness and press it upon the consciences of the hearers. Jonathan Edwards spent hours crafting sermons that brought eternal realities into sharp focus, warning his listeners of the wrath to come and urging them to flee to Christ. The English preacher Charles Spurgeon saturated his sermons with Scripture and doctrinal clarity, exalting Christ above all.

Too many sermons today are structured around felt needs: "How to Reduce Stress," "Three Keys to Better Relationships," or "Finding Your Purpose." These are not necessarily unbiblical topics in themselves, but when Scripture is merely used as a supporting illustration, merely proof-texting a self-help talk, the authority of the text is subordinated to the desires of the audience. The Bible then has been made to serve the self rather than the self being made to submit to the Word of God.

The church no longer knows its own Book when sermons are reduced to self-help advice or motivational encouragements leaving the authority and depth of Scripture suppressed. When the pulpit is replaced by the therapist's couch, God's people are left with little more than spiritual platitudes.

Charles Spurgeon saw in his day what is now full-grown in ours—the replacement of preaching with other things. Spurgeon allegedly warned, "A time will come when instead of shepherds feeding the sheep, the church will have clowns entertaining the goats."[42] In many pulpits today exposition has been displaced by Bible-bites. Sanctuaries resemble theaters; sermons are packaged as motivational speeches or comedic monologues and worship is designed more to excite the senses than to convict the heart. The goal has subtly shifted from feeding the sheep with the Word of God to attracting the goats with spectacle. The self-help, entertainment-driven, sin-denying pulpit may draw a crowd but it cannot produce biblical disciples. It fills empty seats while emptying souls.

Bill Hybels founded Willow Creek Community Church in South Barrington, Illinois in AD 1975 and formulated a seeker-sensitive formula for growth. The church grew to one of the largest megachurches in America. In AD 2007, Bill Hybels made an astonishing apology to the Christian community. After a broad-based study of the church Hybels revealed that "much of what Willow Creek had been doing for over twenty years and promoting to thousands of churches and millions of believers across the globe did not produce sound disciples for Jesus Christ. It produced numbers, but not disciples."[43]

Some of America's most visible megachurches openly brand themselves around the language of entertainment where their worship services rival major music tours than sacred worship. This is precisely the condition Spurgeon foresaw which leaves Christians ignorant of even the most basic doctrines. They may be able to repeat slogans but they cannot articulate the gospel, defend the deity of Christ, or explain why God's holiness demands repentance.

The prophet Hosea spoke to Israel's collapse with words that echo today: "My people are destroyed for lack of knowledge" (Hos 4:6). Without God's Word deeply rooted in their hearts and minds believers become vulnerable to the shifting winds of culture. The old adage: "A Bible that is falling apart usually belongs to someone who isn't" is a truism. Only a return to preaching and teaching that exalts God's Word as supreme can cure the anemia of biblical illiteracy in the church.

The modern church has been weakened not by an external assault but by an internal decay. She has traded the bold proclamation of truth for softer words designed to soothe the conscience rather than to convict of sin. Preaching has been diluted, convictions have been blurred, and biblical literacy has withered under the weight of compromise. In many places, the church has been more eager to please the world than to confront it and more intent on gathering crowds than forming disciples. The result is a generation that knows how to be entertained but not how to endure.

What we have witnessed is not the loss of religion altogether but the loss of its backbone. Where the saints of old risked their lives for the Word of God many today will not risk the disapproval of their peers. Artificialness has replaced authenticity and cowardness has replaced courage.

Yet history has shown us that God does not abandon His people in difficult and turbulent times. Even so, He calls His church today to return to His Word with conviction, boldness, and strength. The path forward will not be found in clever strategies or cultural applause but in the same power that once turned the world upside down—God's people boldly and courageously standing for and proclaiming His Word.

Section III:

The Call to Courage
(The Church Today)

6

The Portrait of Courage

"Do not pray for easy lives; pray to be stronger men."
~ Phillips Brooks

THE CHURCH OF JESUS CHRIST HAS NEVER flourished in comfort but in conflict. From the beginning, the gospel advanced not on beds of ease but on battlefields of faith. History reminds us that the light of God's people shines brightest when it burns against the darkness of the age. The early disciples, when threatened and opposed, did not retreat or ask for safety—they lifted their hearts to heaven and prayed, "Lord, grant to Your servants that with all boldness they may speak Your word" (Acts 4:29). They understood that the measure of their faith was not found in how safe they felt, but in how steadfastly they stood.

The Reformers faced the fury of both pope and prince, standing before kings and councils with nothing but the unshakable Word of God. With trembling hands but fearless hearts, Luther declared, "Here I stand; I can do no other." His courage lit a fire that no earthly power could extinguish. That same flame leapt across oceans to ignite the hearts of believers in the New World. In colonial America, Baptist preachers and laymen endured prison, poverty, and lashings because they believed that Christ's truth was worth every chain and every scar. Their pulpits were not padded with popularity, and their churches were not filled with comfort-seekers, but with men and women who had counted the cost and found Jesus to be worthy of it all.

The story of the Church is a story of courageous obedience. When the world demanded silence, God's people spoke. When compromise seemed easier, they stood firm. When fear whispered retreat, faith shouted advance. Every generation has faced its own furnace, and in each, a remnant has risen who would rather suffer with Christ than succeed without Him. We are now that generation. The trials may look different, but the call is the same.

So, the question before us is not whether times are dark—they always have been. The question is whether we will stand as they did. Will we, too, go against the grain of culture, holding fast to truth when it costs us? Will we live with the same holy resolve that made saints and martyrs unshakeable?

If the contemporary church has been marked by

compromise to the world and timidity in the face of hostility, then the way forward must be marked by conviction and fortitude. God does not call His people to retreat but to stand fast in the Lord and in the power of His might (Eph 6:10). The same Lord who said, "In the world you will have tribulation; but be of good cheer. I have overcome the world" (John 16:33), summons His church today to take up the mantle of courageous faith once more. In every age God has preserved His witness through men and woman who feared Him more than they feared man. Our day requires the same strength of heart.

During the dark years of Nazi Germany many pastors chose silence while others chose outright allegiance to Adolf Hitler. But Dietrich Bonhoeffer, a young Lutheran pastor and theologian, refused to surrender to the authoritarian demands of Hitler. He joined the Confessing Church, a movement that resisted state control of the German church and denounced Hitler's perversion of both politics and religion.

Bonhoeffer's courage was not theatrics in this troubling time. In AD 1939 he had the opportunity to remain safely in the United States, far from the horrors of war and the Nazi regime. Instead, he returned to Germany and wrote to his fellow pastor, Reinold Niebuhr: "I have come to the conclusion that I made a mistake in coming to America. I must live through this difficult period of our national history with the people of Germany. I will have no right to participate in the reconstruction of Christian life in Germany after the war if I do not share in this time of trials with my people."[44]

Bonhoeffer's resistance eventually led him to participate in a plot to assassinate Hitler. He was arrested in AD 1943 and spent two years in prison continuing to preach Christ to his fellow inmates. Even in his final hours his faith and courage stood strong. On April 9, AD 1945, just weeks before Germany's surrender, Bonhoeffer was executed at Flossenbürg concentration camp. A witness, the camp doctor, later testified: "I saw Pastor Bonhoeffer, before taking off his prison garb, kneeling on the floor praying fervently to his God. I was most deeply moved by the way this lovable man prayed, … In the almost fifty years that I worked as a doctor, I have hardly ever seen a man die so entirely submissive to the will of God."[45] Bonhoeffer's life and death became a rallying cry for postwar believers. His book, *The Cost of Discipleship*, still challenges Christians today with the stark reminder, "When Christ calls a man, he bids him come and die."

Another portrait of courage occurred on January 8, AD 1956, when five missionaries, Jim Elliot, Nate Saint, Ed McCully, Pete Fleming, and Roger Youderian, were speared to death on a sandy riverbank in Ecuador by the very tribe they had come to reach with the gospel. Their story shocked the world. *Life* magazine ran a ten-page photo spread under the headline "Missionaries Slain in Jungle" that brought the tragedy into millions of American homes.[46] Many people outside the church saw this tragedy as a waste but believers recognized it as a testimony that Christ is worth more than life itself.

Jim Ellioit had written in his journal just a few years earlier, "He is no fool who gives what he cannot keep to gain what he cannot lose."[47] These words, obscure at the time, became immortal after his death. The world believed these men had lost everything. In reality they gained what could never be taken away.

What happened next stunned the world even further. Within months after these missionaries' deaths, Elisabeth Elliot (Jim's widow) and Rachel Saint (sister of Nate Saint) returned to the Waodani people. Instead of these two ladies going with bitterness, hate, and vengeance at the death of their loved ones, they brought the gospel to them. Unbelievably and against all odds, the very men who had killed the missionaries eventually repented of their sin and came to Christ.[48] The conversion of Mincaye, one of the attackers, stands as a monument to the power of grace. He later became a Christian elder and baptized some of the missionaries' children in the same river where blood had once been shed.[49]

Far from extinguishing missionary zeal, the deaths of

the five martyrs ignited a movement. Young men and women across America and Europe offered themselves to global missions. Enrollment in Bible colleges and seminaries swelled and missionary sending agencies reported a surge in candidates eager to go and share the gospel to unreached peoples.[50]

The commitment by these Christians to take the gospel to the ends of the earth was not simply a curiously hazardous journey for its own sake but a conviction anchored in eternity. These five men did not live their lives recklessly but in obedience. Their sacrifices were the living embodiment of Christ's promise, "For whoever desires to save his life will lose it, but whoever loses his life for My sake will find it" (Matt 16:25). Their legacy continues to preach long after their voices were silenced. The kingdom of God does not advance through safety and convenience but through fearless faith that counts Christ worthy of everything.

Martin Luther King is primarily remembered as a civil rights leader but he was first and foremost a Baptist pastor whose activism followed directly from his Christian convictions. At a time when segregation was the entrenched law of the South, King preached that the gospel demanded both justice and sacrificial love. His resolve is perhaps best captured during his imprisonments. While confined in a Birmingham jail in April AD 1963 for leading nonviolent protests, King penned his famous "Letter from Birmingham Jail." Responding to fellow clergymen who urged patience and caution he wrote, "There was a time when the church was very powerful ... In those days the church was not merely a thermometer that recorded the ideas and principles of popular opinion; it was a thermostat that transformed the mores of society."[51] King's willingness to suffer rather than compromise gave moral authority to his message. His home was bombed, he faced continual threats and he endured repeated arrests. Yet, he remained steadfast in nonviolence.

On April 4, AD 1968, Martin Luther King was assassinated in Memphis, Tennessee, sealing his testimony with his life. Though he was not a missionary in the traditional sense of the word, King exemplified a fearless Christian witness in the public square, declaring that obedience to Christ required confronting injustice even at the cost of his life.

Outside of America we see a portrait of courage and endurance by a man named Aleksandr Solzhenitsyn. In the Soviet Union where communism sought to erase God from public life, Aleksandr Solzhenitsyn became a voice of truth in the face of crushing repression. A decorated officer in the Red Army during World War II, Solzhenitsyn was arrested in AD 1945 for criticizing Stalin in private correspondence. He spent years in prison camps and exile enduring harsh conditions that broke many men. Yet it was in the gulag that he became a Christian and where his faith sustained him with the conviction that truth was worth any cost of suffering.

His monumental work, *The Gulag Archipelago*, exposed to the world the brutal and inhumane treatment of the Soviet labor camps. His work was smuggled to the West and subsequentially published in AD 1973. It became a devastating indictment of a communistic regime built on lies. In his Nobel Prize Lecture in AD 1970 that was delivered *in absentia* he declared, "One word of truth shall outweigh the whole world."[52]

When Aleksandr Solzhenitsyn stepped to the podium at Harvard in AD 1978, many of the elite in the West expected a grateful refugee's praise of democracy and the free world. Instead, he boldly delivered a stinging rebuke warning the West that it too was rotting from within. "A decline in courage may be the most striking feature that an outside observer notices in the West in our days," he declared.[53]

The courage of that moment was not only in what he said but in where he said it. Solzhenitsyn risked his reputation and alienation by speaking truth they did not want to hear. He showed that courage is not only surviving the gulag but daring to confront complacency with the piercing light of truth. This conviction came from more than literary idealism; it is rooted in Christian belief that truth reflects the character of God Himself.

Columbine High School in Littleton, Colorado was the site of one of the deadliest school shootings in American history. On April 20, AD 1999, two students entered the school carrying firearms and bombs and murdered twelve classmates and a teacher before taking their own lives. In the chaos of those hours, testimonies of courage and faith under fire emerged of students who stood for Christ even at gunpoint.

One story that echoed around the world was that of Cassie Bernall, a seventeen-year old student. According to eyewitness accounts, one of the shooters pointed a gun at her and asked if she believed in God. Cassie answered, "Yes." She was then shot and killed instantly.[54] Another student, Rachel Joy Scott, was also killed after giving witness to her faith in Christ. Her journals revealed a young woman who had prayed that God would use her life to reach others, even if it cost her everything.[55]

The stories of Cassie and Rachel became rallying cries for a generation of young believers. Whether every detail of their final moments was recorded with precision or not, what cannot be denied is that they lived and died with a clear testimony of devotion to Christ. Their examples of courage and faith, like those of martyrs through the centuries, remind us that the call to faithfulness is not confined to distant mission fields or oppressive regimes. Sometimes it is demanded in the ordinary spaces of everyday life—even in an American high school.

Another story of standing for truth and having great courage in a hostile world is the story of Jack Phillips. In AD 2012, Jack Phillips, owner of Masterpiece Cakeshop in Lakewood, Colorado, was asked to design a custom wedding cake for a same-sex ceremony. As a Christian, Phillips believed that marriage is ordained by God as the union of one man and one woman. He politely declined the request, offering to sell the couple any other item in his store but explaining that to craft a cake celebrating their wedding would violate his conscience and his faith.

What followed was a storm that has lasted more than a decade. The Colorado Civil Rights Commission ruled against him, ordering him to provide cakes for same-sex weddings and to undergo "re-education." Phillips endured death threats, protests outside his shop, and years of litigation. The case reached the United States Supreme Court, which in AD 2018 ruled 7–2 in his favor, finding that the Colorado commission had displayed "hostility toward his sincere religious beliefs."

Yet the battles did not end there. New lawsuits were filed against him, including one demanding he create a cake celebrating a gender transition. Through it all, Phillips has remained steadfast, refusing to compromise his convictions for the sake of cultural approval or financial security. In his own words: "I serve everybody, but I cannot create custom cakes that express messages that conflict with my deeply held beliefs."[56]

Jack Phillips's story is a reminder that boldness is not only demanded on distant mission fields or in times of war, but in the ordinary callings of life, in workplaces, schools, and neighborhoods where Christians are pressured to bow to the spirit of the age. His stand shows that courage today may look like faithfulness in business, quiet but unyielding, holding fast to the truth even when the cost is lawsuits, threats, and public scorn.

America was shocked once again on September 10, AD 2025, when social media "blew up" and television programming was interrupted with the news that Charlie Kirk, a Christian conservative advocate, had been shot at a "Prove Me Wrong" event at Utah Valley University. Charlie Kirk's life is a modern example of courage and conviction in the face of opposition.

He founded *Turning Point USA*, a movement dedicated to equipping young conservatives on college campuses. He stood for fixed truth in an age of moral relativism rejecting the prevailing cultural winds and reminded audiences that right and wrong are not matters of shifting opinion but of eternal principle. In doing so, he deliberately stepped into one of the most hostile environments imaginable for his worldview. Universities had long been dominated by radical liberal ideas, yet Kirk was willing to stand before hostile audiences, often debating those who disagreed with him most vehemently.

This kind of courage is not without its costs. Standing for truth is not without risk. In an age when compromise is common and courage and conviction are not, Charlie Kirk was willing to count the cost and even pay the supreme price regarding the maxim "the truth shall set you free" (John 8:32).

Whether it is from a jungle riverbank in Ecuador or a Birmingham jail, a Soviet labor camp or the hallways of an American high school, the store of a small bakery business or a university campus, the testimony of courage and faith has been the same—Christ is worth more than life. These people did not set out to be heroes. They were ordinary men and women who answered an extraordinary call to stand for truth without shame and courage in the face of hostility and hatred if necessary.

Their lives press this important question upon us; will we be silent in an age of compromise or will we stand true to the Word of God in the faith once delivered to the saints (Jude 3)? The examples of these faithful individuals remind us that boldness is not an optional virtue but a necessary mark of discipleship. There will always be that pull from culture to compromise.

The call before the modern church is clear. We must recover our voice to proclaim the Word of God with passion and courage and live with the steadfast conviction in a world that demands silence and softness. The world does not need a church that blends in but one that courageously stands out for the truth with love and grace; not a church masked but a church marked by holy boldness.

7

The Gospel in a Hostile Climate

*"The Gospel offends the natural man,
but it saves his soul."* ~ Leonard Ravenhill

THE GOSPEL OF JESUS CHRIST HAS NEVER BEEN A message crafted to win the world's applause. It was not meant to charm the masses or fit neatly into the cultural fashions of the age. From the beginning, it has stood as a divine declaration to confront our sin, our pride, and arrogance. The gospel exposes the darkness of the human heart and calls men and women to humble themselves and repent before the Lordship of Jesus Christ. It does not flatter the ego; it crucified it. It does not celebrate man's wisdom; it reveals it as folly. And because it refuses to exalt man, the world has always resisted it.

To preach such a gospel is to enter the age-old conflict between truth and error; light and darkness; good and evil. Every generation has its idols, its golden calves, dressed in new attire. In the first century Christians faced the multiple gods of the Roman empire; in later centuries, they resisted the worship of images and ecclesiastical power. The Enlightenment exalted human reason above divine revelation, and our own modern age has crowned self as sovereign. The forms have changed but the human heart of rebellion has remained the same. The gospel always cuts across the grain of every culture that seeks to enthrone man instead of God.

Our Lord taught his disciples this reality: "If the world hates you, you know that it hated Me before it hated you" (John 15:18). The early Christians learned quickly that the message of the cross was life-giving but it was also offensive. The Apostle Paul stated, "For we are to God the fragrance of Christ among those who are being saved and among those who are perishing. To the one we are the aroma of death leading to death, and to the other the aroma of life leading to life" (2 Cor 2:15-16). Those early believers were not praised as outstanding citizens, but were labeled as disturbers of the peace and even enemies of the state. Efforts to silence and stamp them out through beatings, imprisonment, and even death were not effective but rather backfired, causing the gospel to be spread more widely.

This has been the testimony of history throughout the ages. The gospel has never thrived in the sunshine of cultural acceptance but in the storms of opposition. The gospel has advanced in every generation from the times of the early church to the present because it has been faithfully proclaimed with boldness whatever the cost. Every effort made by those opposed to the gospel message to censure it or stamp it out has only resulted in the gospel moving farther and faster throughout the world.

The same cultural pressures the early church faced are the same pressures faced today. Our culture demands tolerance where God demands truth. Modern culture applauds compromise and calls it kindness but scorns eternal truths and calls it hate. It tells the church to keep her message private, within the walls of the church building or the homes of believers, and that it is not welcome in the public square. The critics opine that, for the church to be relevant and accepted by the culture, she must accommodate the shifting sands of morality and virtue. Yet, Ps 119:89 declares, "Forever, O Lord, Your word is settled in heaven," which emphasizes the eternal and unchanging nature of God's Word. To dilute the gospel is to destroy it. To proclaim it fully is to unleash its saving power.

The gospel is not a do-it-yourself kind of message where you can earn your way into heaven. It is not even a self-help tip or motivational poster with a Bible verse referenced. The gospel is God's declaration of truth and grace that announces both a guilty verdict and a solution.

It tells the truth about our sin with uncomfortable honesty and it offers hope that is steadfast and sure.

Going all the way back to Adam and Eve in the Garden of Eden we discover that humanity has preferred autonomy over obedience (Genesis 3). Sin is not simply a cosmic blemish; it is moral rebellion that corrupts our lives, distorts our motives, and brings death (Rom 3:9-23). The prophet Jeremiah calls the human heart "deceitful" (Jer 17:9). That is not exactly a compliment but it is an accurate description. Our problem is not merely education or environment; it is guilt before a holy God. God in His holiness hates all workers of iniquity and "no evil shall dwell with You" (Ps 5:4). God's wrath is not an outburst of temper but His settled opposition to all that is evil. God's law exposes every person as guilty and silences every excuse we make. It functions as a mirror to reveal our sinful condition, not as a ladder so we can climb out of it.

If that sounds harsh or severe it is because it is a hard truth. The gospel confronts our sin by exposing our true condition. The gospel is not a message to us to try harder but tells us we cannot save ourselves. This is bad news for our pride but it is good news for us sinners. The heart of the gospel is the substitutionary death on Calvary's cross and victorious resurrection of Jesus Christ. Jesus bore our sins on the cross and died in our place. This sacrifice satisfied the justice of God and in His mercy offers us His righteousness. He redeemed us from the bondage of our sin and set us free to live for Him. His glorious resurrection gave us victory over death and the promises that we too will rise from the grave at His return.

The gospel offers real hope for mankind. This is not wishful thinking; it is a blood-bought reality that is confirmed by His resurrection. The gospel changes lives and gives us genuine hope. To the self-righteous it topples arrogance and levels us all at the foot of the cross. To the sexually broken it offers cleansing and healing. To the greedy it transforms attitudes that opens both the heart and the hand. The gospel offers hope for all mankind because all have sinned.

This hope is meant to be lived out in the world through the church where the Word of God is preached and the believers encourage one another to good works. The church is to be the centerpiece of society as a beacon of light shining brightly in a dark world. It is the "pillar and ground of the truth" (1 Tim 3:15) declaring boldly the unchanging Word of God. God did not design Christianity where we are all on our own against the world, but He founded the local church to be the center of this evangelistic enterprise where we work together to take the gospel to the world.

For much of Western history, gospel-centered evangelism was carried out within those cultures that were at least nominally Christian. Much of the culture had been shaped by the Christian ethos. Today however, our age has been described as a post-Christian age; a time when Christian assumptions by previous generations no longer hold sway. Today is an age when skepticism of faith is high, truth is seen as relative and not absolute, and biblical authority is too often rationalized away. Yet the Great Commission has not been rescinded. If anything, the task of proclaiming Christ in such an environment is more urgent and more challenging. Evangelism in this "cultural moment" requires courage and discernment as believers must remember that the gospel itself remains unchanged even when the surrounding culture has shifted.

A post-Christian society does not mean the absence of religion. Rather it is one that has moved beyond Christian influence and often has deliberately rejected it. This differs from pre-Christian paganism where the gospel was an entirely new message in the culture. In post-Christian settings the gospel is often viewed as something tried, found ineffective, or even oppressive. This creates both unique obstacles and surprising opportunities for evangelism. The modern hearer often thinks they already know about Christianity but their knowledge is too often shallow, distorted or shaped by cultural caricatures. As G. K. Chesterton famously said, "The Christian ideal has not been tried and found wanting. It has been found difficult; and left untried."[57] The challenge is not simply to introduce

Jesus as if for the first time but to cut through layers of misunderstanding and show the gospel in its true, life-giving power.

The challenges of evangelism are many. First, biblical cultural amnesia has left large portions of the population ignorant of the most basic biblical stories and themes. Where once references to God's creation in Genesis, the children of Israel being led by Moses out of Egyptian bondage in the Exodus across the Red Sea, the story of Samson and Delilah and his long hair, Jonah being swallowed by the great fish, and the battle between the shepherd boy David fighting against the giant Philistine Goliath were well-known within the culture. Today these biblical stories often fall flat because the hearer is totally ignorant of them.

Second there is a widespread suspicion of authority. This is not only toward the government but also the church. The moral failure of some well-known Christian leaders combined with political entanglements and public scandals have led many to distrust institutional religion altogether. High profile preachers with large social media footprints have been exposed as hypocrites and have tarnished the public perception of all preachers.

Relativism has also taken deep root in the modern West. Postmodernism has penetrated every segment of society from the halls of government to the institutions of learning. Truth is not seen by many as absolute but as the circumstance will dictate. What is true for one person may not be true for someone else. Everyone has their own truth. To claim that Christianity is true and to say that there is an exclusivity of Christ in salvation is often viewed as arrogant, intolerant, and even hateful. Pluralism also plays a role in this mindset because it declares that all beliefs are equally valid and one religion is as good as another because everyone is going to heaven anyway.

Affluence also plays a role in the challenges of evangelism today. Affluence tends to dull spiritual hunger because the affluent seem to have everything and need nothing. Many do not reject Christ outright; they simply never stop to consider Him because they are totally absorbed in their own comfort and entertainment. These challenges demand that the Church think carefully about her approach without watering down her message.

Even as the culture shifts, the biblical anchors for evangelism remain firm. The New Testament itself was written into a pluralistic, hostile world. The Apostle Paul preached Christ in pagan Athens at Mars Hill (Acts 17), Peter addressed scattered believers under persecution (1 Peter 1), and John reminded churches of the conquering Lamb (Revelation 1). These offer timeless lessons to every age. Evangelism must remain centered on the message of Christ. It is not mere moral reform, cultural preservation, or a call to vague spirituality. It is the announcement of Christ crucified and risen as Paul declared: "Moreover, brethren, I declare to you the gospel which I preached to you, which you also received and in which you stand. ... For I delivered to you first of all that which I also received, that Christ died for our sins according to the Scriptures, and that He was buried, and that He rose again the third day according to the Scriptures" (1 Cor 15:1–4).

Christians are to embody the gospel as they proclaim it. The culture needs to witness the lifestyle and authenticity of Christians to give credibility of the gospel to the hearers. Evangelism does not simply rely on human persuasion but on the power of God. This conviction must undergird every effort in evangelism. As Paul wrote, "For I am not ashamed of the gospel of Christ, for it is the power of God to salvation for everyone who believes, for the Jew first and also for the Greek" (Rom 1:16).

Strategies for evangelism in a post-Christian age vary widely, however, first and foremost there must be a recovery of gospel centrality. The temptation to dilute or conform the message to suit modern tastes must be resisted. While methods may vary, the message must remain the same.

Some who verbalize the maxim "methods change but not the message" in practice are actually altering the message. In seeker-sensitive services the worship is primarily formatted for the lost and unchurched to keep them coming. The preaching in those services is designed to not offend, yet the biblical gospel is offensive. That does not mean the gospel should be delivered crudely without regard for others, but it is to be delivered honestly and with clarity. In this skeptical age authenticity is one of the most powerful apologetics. Christians must live out their faith without reproach, giving their message credibility which mere words cannot supply.

Modern evangelism must engage both the mind and heart. Apologetics that answer intellectual objections are necessary but genuine compassion that addresses emotional wounds is important as well. Truth without love can harden; love without truth can deceive. The age-old maxim "I don't care how much you know until I know how much you care" is important in evangelism.

Personal testimonies, biblical narratives, and even modern stories of transformation help make the gospel real and relatable. This enables evangelism to be lived out in everyday places as ordinary Christians live faithful lives in their neighborhoods, workplaces, and online communities. Salt and light work quietly but persistently influencing by presence as much as by proclamation.

History provides encouragement for this task. Every era has faced unique challenges to evangelism. The early church thrived despite Roman hostility, growing rapidly even when marginalized or persecuted. The Reformers proclaimed the gospel against entrenched church corruption and risked their lives for its truth. The revivalists of the eighteenth and nineteenth centuries preached amidst widespread apathy and moral decline, sparking awakenings that transformed entire societies. Each generation believed their moment was uniquely difficult, yet the Spirit of God proved sufficient. The post-Christian West, with all its skepticism and hostility, is not beyond His reach. If anything, the absence of cultural Christianity may purify the witness of the Church, forcing believers to rely more fully on God's power and less on cultural momentum.

Evangelism in a post-Christian culture may be harder in some respects than previous times, but it also can give a greater contrast. The church can no longer depend on inherited societal morality, or nominal Christian faith, or societal respectability. It must return to the fundamentals of the faith – Christ crucified, the call to repentance and faith, and the Holy Spirit's power to transform lives. In such a post-Christian world, evangelism will demand courage, patience, and love but it will also shine all the brighter against the darkness. The very obstacles of this age may become the stage upon which the glory of God is most clearly displayed. The believer's responsibility to witness has not changed and the gospel has not lost its power. What is required is a faithful, uncompromising, bold witness that points a weary soul to the only true source of life, Jesus Christ the Lord. Even in this difficult age, hearts remain restless and the age-old gospel still answers the deepest needs of every generation. When the church stands firm in the Word of God and loves others as themselves, God continues to draw people out of darkness and into His marvelous light.

8

Standing Together: Courage in Community

"Though none go with me, still I will follow."
~ Hymn: "I Have Decided to Follow Jesus"

WHEN WE THINK OF COURAGE, OUR MINDS often picture the lone hero like the prophet who stands unflinching before a defiant king, or the martyr who refuses to deny Christ though the tribunal rages against him, or the solitary pastor who will not compromise God's Word no matter the pressure. Those scenes stir our hearts because they remind us that courage has a cost and that truth often stands alone. Yet if we stop there, we miss something vital. Christian courage is not just the story of isolated heroes; it is the story of a faithful people.

From the very beginning, the church has been a fellowship of the brave. Courage has never been an exclusive individual virtue but a shared grace, a holy boldness that grows stronger in the company of the redeemed. The early believers stood shoulder to shoulder under persecution and prayed together when threatened. They sang in union behind prison bars. The Spirit of God knit them together in steadfast faith. Courage multiplied in community, and their unity became their corporate testimony.

The book of Acts shows us this very clearly. From the moment the Spirit descended at Pentecost, believers began to live and speak with a fearlessness that astonished their world. When Peter and John stood before the Sanhedrin, they did not cower, for they had already been strengthened by the prayers of the believing community. When the church faced threats, they did not scatter in fear but gathered to pray, and "the place where they were assembled together was shaken; and they were all filled with the Holy Spirit and they spoke the word of God with boldness" (Acts 4:31). The courage of one became the courage of all. Their boldness was not born of human resolve but of divine unity, a church filled and empowered by the Spirit of God.

Church history echoes this biblical pattern. The Waldensians huddled together in Alpine valleys reciting Scripture to one another, drawing courage from their fellowship as they faced harsh persecution from both church and state. The English Separatists in the 16th and

17th centuries gathered in secret to strengthen one another with psalms, hymns, and corporate prayers when imprisonment or death loomed at the door. Colonial Baptists in America endured fines, brutal beatings, and jail sentences, not as isolated victims but as congregations that rallied behind their persecuted and imprisoned pastors, sometimes even gathering outside the jail windows to sing hymns and encourage the one suffering for their shared faith. In every era, when one believer stood others also soon found the strength to join him.

This is no less true today. Courage in our day must not stand alone; it must rise within the fellowship of God's people. The lone believer may spark a flame, but only a faithful community can keep it burning. We live in a culture that celebrates heightened individualism and the autonomy of self. Too many people today are isolated from the very relationships that are designed to give them strength. Too many professing Christians attempt to live out their faith in isolation cut off from the life of the local church. The result is very predictable resulting in discouragement, compromise, bitterness, and collapse. But when believers stand shoulder to shoulder with each other they are far stronger than the sum of their parts. The fire of one heart can ignite a congregation. The unified prayers of a congregation can uphold the solitary witness.

This truth is simple, but it is urgent: courage grows in fellowship. The fires of faith burn brightest when believers stand together. That is why Scripture warns us to "not forsake the assembling of ourselves together, as is the manner of some, but exhorting one another, and so much the more as you see the Day approaching" (Heb 10:25). Isolation weakens us; community strengthens us. A single coal pulled from the fire soon grows cold, but when joined with the others it glows with renewed heat; so it is with courage in the Christian life.

A Christian standing alone may falter, but a church standing together cannot be ignored. The world may dismiss one voice, but it cannot silence a united chorus of faith. We need one another's prayers when fear whispers in the dark. We need one another's presence when the battle feels long and weary. We need one another's encouragement when the culture mocks conviction and when the cost of obedience feels high. This is why the New Testament church prayed together, wept together, sang together, and suffered together. Sharing each other's burdens lifted each other's faith.

What the world needs most today is not a shattering of brave individuals, but a strong gathering of steadfast believers. We need churches that refuse to bend in fear and stand together in boldness and faith. We need congregations unashamed to stand against the trend, to pray down the fear that grips their pastors, to lift up the fainthearted, and to remind one another that the gospel is still worth every cost. In a hostile world, courage in community is not optional, it is essential. Without it, we will grow timid; with it, we will stand firm until Christ returns.

In Nazi Germany, Martin Niemöller stood against Hitler's attempt to seize control of the Lutheran church. Once sympathetic to the new regime, Niemöller soon realized that Christ could not share His throne with the Führer. In AD 1937, Niemöller was arrested and confined first in Berlin's Tegel Prison, then in the concentration camps of Sachsenhausen and Dachau. From the outside, it looked like a solitary man crushed under state power. Yet within the bars of confinement, Niemöller knew he was not alone. The *Confessing Church*, that fragile band of courageous pastors and congregations who refused to compromise, prayed for him continually and spread his sermons and continued to preach Christ with costly defiance. Their solidarity gave him strength. Niemöller later testified that the courage of the body outside the prison walls sustained the man behind them.[58]

The same dynamic unfolded two decades later in Montgomery, Alabama. Rosa Parks's quiet defiance on a segregated bus in December AD 1955 could have ended in silence and obscurity had it not been for the church. Black congregations immediately rallied, filling sanctuaries with prayer, song, and sermon that transformed one woman's stand into a people's movement. Black leaders organized a citywide protest and together they refused to ride the public buses sparking what became known as the Montgomery Bus Boycott. Churches organized carpools to replace buses, held nightly gatherings to renew strength, and reminded worshippers that God's justice was greater than man's laws. Parks herself was lifted by this network of faith; her personal courage became effective only because it was reinforced by the body around her.[59]

Behind the Iron Curtain, the same truth was written in harsher ink. Richard Wurmbrand, a Lutheran pastor in communist Romania, refused to publicly support communism and was arrested by the secret police for preaching the gospel. He spent fourteen years in prison, three of them in solitary confinement. Despite beatings, starvation, and psychological torture he remained steadfast. Yet even in his resistance, it was not his alone. His congregation defied the authorities, gathered in secret, and cared for his wife Sabina and their son after his arrest. Smuggling food, providing shelter, and sharing prayers under surveillance, they bore the burden with him. Wurmbrand knew he did not suffer alone but drew strength from his church and fellow prisoners as they encouraged one another.[60]

Dietrich Bonhoeffer's testimony reminds us that even before the battle comes, Christian fellowship helps prepare courage. Between AD 1935 and AD 1937, he gathered young pastors into a secret seminary at Finkenwalde, Poland as they resisted the Hitler regime. There they ate, studied, prayed and sang together as they enjoyed life with each other. The Gestapo eventually closed the seminary but the bonds of brotherhood forged there held fast. Many of those men went on to suffer imprisonment and martyrdom themselves, strengthened by the shared courage they had cultivated in community. Bonhoeffer reportedly said, "Silence in the face of evil is itself evil. Not to speak is to speak. Not to act is to act." He was arrested by the Nazi regime for his connections to the resistance. In April AD 1945, just weeks before the war ended, he was executed by hanging at Flossenbürg concentration camp. Bonhoeffer's final act of resistance was born not out of isolation, but of fellowship woven into the fabric of his daily life.[61]

This pattern of corporate strength and prayer sustaining the one continues on. In AD 2016, Andrew Brunson, an American pastor serving in Turkey, was falsely accused of espionage and locked away for two years. Alone in a cell, he battled despair and panic, confessing later that he feared his faith would break. Yet all around the world, congregations and prayer groups lifted him up before the throne of grace. Vigils were held, letters were sent, and believers in Turkey encouraged his wife when she too faced government pressure. Brunson would later write that the knowledge of the church's prayers helped sustain him. His release in AD 2018 was not only an answer to prayer but a testimony that when one suffers, the whole body suffers with him, and when one stands the whole body stands with him.[62]

These are a few examples that courage at its root is not a solitary virtue. The picture of the lone Christian standing bravely before the powers of the time is stirring but it is incomplete. The Lord never designed His people to walk the narrow road alone. Even when courage appears in one individual, it is almost always the fruit of a core group of believers standing behind him. From the beginning, God's design has been that His people would endure together. As the wise preacher in Ecclesiastes reminds us, "Two are better than one ... and a threefold cord is not quickly broken" (Eccl 4:9–12). This is not sentimentality but God's blueprint for resilience and strength.

The New Testament church confirms this truth as well. When Peter and John were arrested for preaching Christ, they did not retreat into isolation. Instead, they sought out their brothers and sisters and lifted their voices in prayer to God. Luke records that "when they had prayed, the place where they were assembled together was shaken; and they were all filled with the Holy Spirit, and they spoke the word of God with boldness" (Acts 4:31). The shaking did not come before the prayer meeting but after it. Boldness was not born in the solitary cell but in the gathered body.

Paul echoes the same call to the Philippians, urging them to "stand fast in one spirit, with one mind striving together for the faith of the gospel" (Phil 1:27). Notice that Paul does not speak to isolated individuals, but to a body. He knew that courage, when practiced together, becomes a fortress against fear. The writer of Hebrews makes the same point, "And let us consider one another in order to stir up love and good works, not forsaking the assembling of ourselves together, as the manner of some, but exhorting one another, and so much the more as you see the Day approaching" (Heb 10:24-25). The Christian draws his strength from the Lord and from the body. Perseverance is sustained in fellowship not in isolation.

What does this look like in practical terms? It looks like when believers meet together to pray courage is buttressed and fear is broken. The early church shook buildings because they first shook heaven with their prayers (Acts 4:23-31). It looks like Christians who are willing to bear one another's burdens in tangible ways (Gal 6:2). A church of believers who surrounds its suffering members with visible, costly support, is a community that fosters endurance. It looks like practicing faithfulness in ordinary commitments. Churches that are consistent in ordinary discipleship are the ones prepared for greater trials. And it looks like congregations that sing, pray, and study God's Word together are strengthened in the gospel and prepared to stand boldly for truth in a challenging world.

This is why Paul's closing words to the Corinthian congregation are still applicable today where he wrote, "Watch, stand fast in the faith, be brave, be strong" (1 Cor 16:13). This is a summons to steadfastness addressed to the church as a body. Christ has so designed His people that they are unshakable when joined together locally under Him as the Head.

Christ's churches should close ranks in the fellowship. They are to stand with those who suffer for Christ and pray together until fear gives way to faith. God's churches should encourage one another and stand united against the enemy that would destroy her. When believers live and suffer in community courage does not fail but grows stronger in the Lord who will never leave them nor forsake them.

Section IV:

Fueling the Flame
(Where Courage Comes From)

9

Biblical Foundations for Courage

"Have I not commanded you? Be strong and of good courage; do not be afraid, nor be dismayed, for the Lord your God is with you wherever you go." ~ Joshua 1:9

WE ARE LIVING IN A TIME WHEN FEAR HAS become like the air we breathe. Courage seems rare, while caution and compromise are treated as if they were the highest of virtues. To remain silent is now called wisdom and to keep one's head down is now praised as maturity. But deep down, we know the truth. Much of what is passed off as prudence in the church today is nothing more than cowardice dressed up in church clothes.

The evidence is all around us and one can feel it in the atmosphere. Many pulpits that once thundered with "Thus says the Lord," are now tiptoeing around the edges of truth worried that a sharp word might empty a pew. Congregations are increasingly being molded by the world's standards rather than shaping the culture with God's Word. In churches and denominations where conviction once burned brightly, we now find leaders carefully calibrating their words as not to offend, sometimes even apologizing for having held to the very truths that once defined the faith. And in the everyday lives of believers there seems to be a quiet hesitancy, even a shrinking back, when the name of Christ ought to be lifted high. This is what an age of cowardice looks like.

Fear is natural but faith can transform fear into boldness and courage. The Word of God speaks into our fear with a different voice. To Joshua, trembling on the edge of the Promised Land, God declared, "Have I not commanded you? Be strong and of good courage; do not be afraid, nor be dismayed, for the Lord your God is with you wherever you go" (Josh 1:9). That refrain, "Do not be afraid" echoes throughout the pages of Scripture. From Abraham to Isaiah, from the disciples on a storm-tossed sea to the Apostle John exiled on the isle of Patmos, the same command is given, fear not, for the Lord is near.

This is the foundation for Christian courage. It is not arrogance nor reckless abandon, but a steady conviction that the presence of God outweighs the threats of men. In an hour when the world applauds silence and punishes conviction, the people of God must rediscover this bedrock truth: our courage flows not from ourselves but from the unshakable promises of the One who said, "I will never leave you nor forsake you" (Heb 13:5).

The command to "fear not" is one of the most repeated messages in all of Scripture. It is as though the Lord knew how easily our hearts would tremble and how prone we would be to discouragement. Like a loving father calming the heart of a frightened child, God again and again whispers into the hearts of His children, "Do not be afraid." This calming assurance is sounded forth from Genesis to Revelation, from the patriarchs to the apostle. The call is always the same, the people of God are not to be controlled by fear. Why is this? Because the presence of God with us, along with His power and promises, are greater than every threat we face.

Courage is not simply a matter of temperament. Some men are naturally bolder than others. Some thrive in danger while others shrink back from conflict. But the courage to which Scripture calls us is not personality driven. It is biblical to its core. True Christian courage flows not from human strength but from who God is and what He has promised as He is present with His people. It is walking in faith not in fear.

The strongest foundation for courage is the steadfast presence of God. Every instance in Scripture where God is at work in the lives of His children His presence is with them. Whether it is Joshua, Moses, the prophets or apostles, King David expresses this truth in the beautiful twenty-third Psalm, "Yea, though I walk through the valley of the shadow of death, I will fear no evil; For You are with me" (Ps 23:4).

God's presence is no less with us today, for Jesus Himself gave us this promise, "Lo, I am with you always, even to the end of the age" (Matt 28:20). There is the faithful assurance that there is no attack too hostile, no culture too dark, no trial too heavy where Christ is not standing with His people. The awareness of His presence can transform fear into fearlessness.

When human strength falters and human resources run dry, the power of the Lord is mighty. Isaiah records the word of God to His fearful people, "Fear not, for I am with you; be not dismayed, for I am your God. I will strengthen you, yes, I will help you. I will uphold you with My righteous right hand" (Isa 41:10). Notice the verbs: God *strengthens*, God *helps*, God *upholds*. Courage is not gritting our teeth and mustering enough willpower to stand, it is relying on the power of Almighty God.

We see this truth reinforced throughout the New Testament. Paul, who faced prisons, beatings, and constant threats, confessed his own weakness but also testified to the enabling power of God, "I can do all things through Christ who strengthens me" (Phil 4:13). His courage was not born out of his strong personality but from a strong Savior. Paul knew that God's grace was sufficient and God's strength was made perfect in Paul's weakness (2 Cor 12:9). The weaker Paul felt, the stronger Christ proved to be.

The sure foundation of the promises of God wrap up this trilogy for the basis of courage. Fear often thrives in uncertainty. When we cannot see what lies ahead or are unsure of possible outcomes, fear may take hold. Yet the promises of God are sufficient to anchor their souls. God's promise to never leave us or forsake us (Heb 13:5) is the basis where we can boldly declare, "The Lord is my helper; I will not fear. What can man do to me?" (Heb 13:6). Courage is the fruit of faith planted in the unfailing promises of God.

Even in the face of death, believers can cling to the sweet promise of Jesus, "I am the resurrection and the life. He who believes in Me, though he may die, he shall live" (John 11:25). The martyrs of Christian history, from Stephen down through the centuries, could face the sword and the flame because they believed that death was not the end but the beginning of new life in their eternal home.

This perspective changes everything. If this life is all there is, then it makes sense to cling to comfort and security. But believers have the eternal truth that to be absent from the body is to be present with the Lord (2 Cor 5:8). The Psalmist declared, "The Lord is on my side; I will not fear. What can man do to me?" (Ps 118:6). Courage rises up even in the face of ridicule, opposition, and even death. The fear of man is swallowed up by the fear of God.

In this age of cowardice, when silence is rewarded and conviction is costly, the people of God must return to this bedrock promise, "God has not given us a spirit of fear, but of power and of love and of a sound mind" (2 Tim 1:7). God's Word is our foundation and here is our courage.

One of the most urgent places where courage must be seen today is in the pulpit. When the man of God grows timid, the whole flock is in danger of deception. A pastor who trims his message to please the crowd and dances around sin is like a watchman who sees the enemy coming but refuses to sound the alarm. He may win applause for a moment, but he loses heaven's approval in the process. The call to preach is not a call to popularity, but a call to fidelity. To preach God's Word courageously is to love God's truth more than man's opinion and to trust that His Word will do its work and accomplish its purpose (Isa 55:11).

Courage must be seen not only in what we profess to believe, but in what we are willing to stand for when the pressure mounts. Conviction that never costs anything is not courage, it is convenience. The cultural headwinds are fierce, and the temptation to quietly adjust our beliefs "just a little" can feel almost irresistible. Yet that is how erosion works, not in sudden collapse, but in subtle compromise.

The moral battlegrounds of our day, life in the womb, marriage as God designed it, the God-ordained roles of men and women, and the exclusivity of salvation through Christ, are not political talking points; they are spiritual tests. Each issue draws a clear line between those who will anchor themselves to the Word of God and those who will drift with the current of public opinion.

To contest what God calls sin does not make one enlightened or compassionate; it makes one deceived. To soften the truth for the sake of acceptance is not mercy, it is moral surrender. True compassion never required us to contradict God. Jesus never compromised truth to win the approval of men, yet sinners flocked to Him because they saw in Him both grace and conviction. Love that abandons truth is not love at all, it is sentimentality without substance.

When we call evil what God calls evil, the world may accuse us of hate. But to remain silent while people march toward destruction is the real cruelty. Biblical love warns, corrects, and points to the cross, even when it costs us. Courage means speaking what God has said, even when it is unpopular; standing where Scripture stands, even when it is lonely; and holding convictions not because they are traditional, but because they are true.

Courage at its deepest level is not about revving ourselves up for the challenges of life but in fixing our gaze on the One who walks with us in the storm. When Peter kept his eyes on Christ he walked upon the waves. When he turned and saw the waves he began to sink. The difference was not the size of the storm but the object of his focus; so it is for us. Our courage will rise or fall in proportion to how clearly we see Christ. A fearful church that lifts her eyes to Him will find strength the world cannot comprehend.

History reminds us that the kingdom of God has never advanced by the cautious or the fainthearted. It was not timidity that carried the gospel from Jerusalem to the ends of the earth even down to our time. It was the bravery of men and women more concerned with their obedience to Christ than to their own safety. That same conviction is needed now for the stakes are no less eternal.

The ultimate measure of courage is not found in how loudly we speak or how obstinately we stand but in how faithfully we live. When God's people dare to live with their eyes lifted up and their hearts saturated with His Word, their lives become sermons proclaiming to a fearful world that there is a God who reigns and a Savior who saves.

The question before us is not whether the world will oppose the truth; it always has. The question is whether the church will meet that opposition with trembling silence or steadfast faith. When the church bows to fear, it forfeits its witness. When it stands with Christ, it shakes the world.

May this generation be remembered not for retreat, but for courage—for lives marked by conviction, for churches filled with holy boldness, and for believers who endure with hope, strengthening one another in love, and pressing forward in faithful obedience until faith becomes sight and we stand rejoicing before our glorious King.

10

Spiritual Disciplines of the Courageous

"The Spirit-filled life is not a special, deluxe edition of Christianity. It is part and parcel of the total plan of God for His people." ~ A. W. Tozer

EVERY CHRISTIAN SHOULD HAVE A DESIRE TO grow spiritually, yet many are satisfied with their status quo. They know they should be farther along in their spiritual life and even at times lament that fact, but they are comfortable to be like everyone else. Those who desire to grow often are looking for an express lane to maturity or some quick fix toward Christlikeness. The truth is there is no fast track to growth and it never happens by accident. Spiritual maturity is cultivated by steady, deliberate practice.

Chief among these are the Word of God and prayer. Leonard Ravenhill once warned, "A man who is intimate with God will never be intimidated by men."[63] That intimacy is established in the secret place of devotional life through Scripture and prayer. When the Bible and prayer are woven together the Christian soul is both fed and strengthened. One without the other leaves us unbalanced, as they are like twin oars that keep us rowing toward maturity.

Imagine a man trying to breathe with only one lung. He might survive but he will never thrive as God intended. His chest rises and falls, but with every breath he is straining, unable to draw in the fullness of air his body was designed for. Now, picture the Chrisian who only reads the Bible but seldom prays, or who prays but often neglects the Word. Spiritually, he is living on half capacity. He may get by but he will never walk in the strength and vitality God intended. The reason is the Bible is how God speaks to us and prayer is how we speak back to Him. Together, they form the rhythm of a living, breathing relationship. You cannot know God deeply without both.

A. W. Tozer wrote, "Nothing less than a whole Bible can make a whole Christian."[64] God has ordained that His voice through Scripture and our voice through prayer form the rhythm of our relationship with Him. The Bible is not simply a book of history or good advice; it is the living Word of God (Heb 4:12). It is His voice to us in every age and every generation. When we open its pages, we are not just engaging with ink on paper but we are meeting with the God of all creation who loves us.

Prayer, on the other hand, is our response to the voice of God. It is not meant to be a hurried request but a continued conversation between the Creator and the creature. We are to draw near to God in praise, confession, and thanksgiving, and relish in His presence. James tells us to, "Draw near to God and He will draw near to you" (James 4:8). Together these practices form a dialogue where God speaks and we listen, then we speak and God hears. This rhythm repeated day after day is the way to spiritual maturity.

Every path to Christian maturity begins with Scripture. Peter writes, "As newborn babes, desire the pure milk of the word, that you may grow thereby" (1 Pet 2:2). Just as an infant will not grow without milk, the believer cannot grow without the Word of God. Sadly, many Christians treat Bible reading like taking vitamins, an optional supplement instead of a daily necessity. Is it no wonder many feel their faith to be anemic?

Andrew Murray reminds us, "The entrance of God's Word gives light. Let every experience of God's Word be accompanied by prayer and faith, that it may work effectually in you."[65] Feeding on the Word of God requires more than a hurried scan. It means reading carefully and meditating with prayerful attention. It means asking, What is God saying? What truth is revealed here? What command must I obey? or What promise can I embrace?

It also means slowing down enough to let the Word sink in deeply. The psalmist says, "But his delight is in the law of the LORD, and in His law he meditates day and night" (Ps 1:2). Meditation is the bridge between reading and living. Again, the Psalmist declared, "I will meditate on Your precepts, and contemplate Your ways" (Ps 119:15). The more a person meditates on the Word of God the more the mind of Christ is formed in him.

Picture a farmer walking through his fields at dawn slowly inspecting the soil, the plants, and the fruit. That is meditation; lingering over God's Word, turning it over in the mind and letting it shape how we see life. Without meditation Bible reading becomes like water running through a pipe, flowing in and out but never soaking in.

Spiritual maturity is not proven by how many verses you can quote but by how much Scripture you actually obey. James warns us, "But be doers of the word, and not hearers only, deceiving yourselves" (Jas 1:22). The real test of spiritual maturity is how your life is conformed to the Word of God in obedience. This is why application is so vital. When you read a passage about forgiveness, ask yourself, "Is there someone I need to forgive?" When you come across commands to purify yourself, ask yourself, "Am I harboring a pet sin instead of repenting of it?" When you read about generosity of your material wealth, ask yourself, "Am I hoarding what God has entrusted to me?"

Application is sometimes the most difficult part because it demands more than simply the intellect; it demands surrender. It is one thing to underline a verse of Scripture in the Bible and quite another to let that verse underline you. Obedience often presses into the area of life we would rather fence off but God's Word, like a surgeon's scalpel, cuts precisely where needed. Those who submit to that gracious surgery find freedom and strength they never had before.

Spiritual maturity is not measured by how much Scripture we can quote, but by how much of it we actually live. Growth comes not from collecting truths, but from conforming to them. Every act of obedience stretches our faith and deepens our character. The more we obey, the more like Christ we become.

If the Word of God is food for the soul, then prayer is its breath. When a person stops breathing his life could cease. Stop praying and spiritual vitality withers. Paul's command is simple, "Pray without ceasing (1 Thess 5:17). This does not mean walking around all day muttering prayers under your breath, but it does mean cultivating an attitude of constant dependence upon God.

Prayer is not first about getting things from God, but about drawing near to Him. The pattern our Lord gave in the Sermon on the Mount begins with worship, "Our Father in heaven, hallowed be Your name (Matt 6:9). Before we present our needs to God, we should pause to adore Him for who He is. When we begin this way our hearts are lifted up above the noise of our worries and our thoughts are centered on His greatness. Worship reorders our perspective.

This lesson is seen clearly in Psalm 73, a Psalm of Asaph. He had difficulty making sense of how the wicked prospered (73:3) and they are not in trouble as other men (73:5). Asaph cries out, "Behold, these are the ungodly, who are always at ease; they increase in riches. Surely, I have cleansed my heart in vain, and washed my hands in innocence." He is in despair seeing the injustice around him and so exclaimed, "When I thought how to understand this, it was too painful for me—Until I went into the sanctuary of God, then I understood their end" (73:16–17). Worshipping God changed his perspective and it will ours as well. Private worship is important in our devotional lives but corporate worship is also essential to our spiritual maturity. The writer of the book of Hebrews tells us, "And let us consider one another in order to stir up love and good works, not forsaking the assembling of ourselves together, as is the manner of some, but exhorting one another and so much the more as you see the Day approaching" (Heb 10:24–25).

But prayer is also the place of honesty. Max Lucado gives good advice, "Don't worry about having the right words; worry more about having the right heart. It's not eloquence he seeks, just honesty."[66]

Nothing slows our walk with God more than carrying hidden sin. We must be honest with ourselves and not rationalize our sin. Just as plaque can clog an artery, unconfessed sin clogs the fellowship we have with God and others. David knew this well, "When I kept silent, my bones grew old through my groaning all the day long" (Ps 32:3). Yet in confession, the dam breaks and God's mercy rushes in. "If we confess our sins, He is faithful and just to forgive us our sins and to cleanse us from all unrighteousness" (1 John 1:9). Honest confession clears the channels of the soul and restores sweetness to communion with God.

Petition is also a part of a complete prayer life. Our Father invites us to bring our needs, fears, and even our desires before Him. Jesus assured us, "Ask, and it will be given to you; seek and you will find; knock, and it will be opened to you" (Matt 7:7). But as we mature, our petitions shift from self-centered wishes to God-centered desires. We begin to pray less for comfort and more for holiness, less for our will to be done and more for His.

Finally, prayer is not meant to be an occasional appointment but a continual posture. Paul exhorts us to "pray without ceasing" (1 Thess 5:17). This does not mean we spend every waking hour with bowed head and folded hands, but that we carry a constant awareness of God's presence and talk to Him all day long. Like a child who instinctively runs to his father, the mature believer learns to bring every joy and every trouble to the Lord in real time. Ole Hallesby teaches us, "As impossible as it is for us to take a breath in the morning large enough to last us until noon, so impossible it is to pray in the morning in such a way as to last us until noon ... Let your prayers ascend to Him constantly, audibly or silently, as circumstances throughout the day permit."[67]

Prayer then is not a duty to be checked off, but a continual lifeline to be cherished. In worship, we re-center on God's greatness. In confession, we are cleansed and restored. In petition, we bring our needs unto His will. And in continual dependence, we learn to walk with Him moment by moment. Prayer is the furnace where intimacy with God is kindled and the workshop where spiritual maturity is forged.

The strongest growth happens when Scripture and prayer are woven together in a unity of function. When you read God's Word, let it guide your prayers. For instance, if you read Psalm 23, turn it into a prayer, "Lord, thank You for being my Shepherd. Guide me in Your paths today. Provide what I need and keep me from wandering." This is praying Scripture. Likewise, let prayer prepare your heart for Scripture. Before opening the Bible pray, "Open my eyes, that I may see wondrous things from Your law" (Ps 119:18). Prayer prepares the heart so God's Word can sink deeper.

Many of the giants of the faith grew strong using some form of this method. George Müller, known for his orphan work, was not primarily a man of actions but a man of prayer and the Word. His journals are filled with records of Scripture inspired prayers and the remarkable answers that followed. His life illustrates that the secret to fruitfulness is not clever strategy but deep communion with God. The more Scripture shapes prayer, the more prayer deepens Scripture.

Spiritual maturity is not the product of some secret formula. It is the fruit of consistent fellowship with God through His Word and prayer. Like two oars working together, they keep the Christian life moving forward in steady rhythm. Neglect either one and you will drift; practice both faithfully together and you will grow. Leonard Ravenhill said, "No man is greater than his prayer life."[68] A. W. Tozer echoed, "The man who would truly know God must give time to Him."[69] The giant men of the faith remind us that growth comes not from shortcuts, gimmicks, or spiritual fads, but from long obedience in the same direction.

If you want to mature in Christ, do not look for quick fixes. Plant yourself in Holy Scripture. Breathe deeply in prayer. Day by day, moment by moment, let God's voice shape you and let your voice rise to Him. In due time you will look back and see that He has made you strong, not in yourself, but in Him. And that is what true Christian maturity is all about.

Conclusion:
Will We Be Found Faithful

"Finally, brethren, be strong in the Lord and in the power of His might." ~ Ephesians 6:10

THE PAGES OF CHURCH HISTORY ARE STAINED with the tears, prayers, and the blood of those who walked before us. They were ordinary men and women like ourselves but they had extraordinary resolve who believed that Christ was worthy of their very lives. Some stood before kings, some hid in caves, some preached in pulpits, and some spoke the gospel through prison bars. What united them was not ease, comfort, or cultural applause, but a deep conviction that Jesus Christ is Lord and that His Word is truth. They lived not for the applause of men but for the approval of heaven. And now, the question hangs over our generation: *will we be found faithful?*

We stand at the hinge of history. Every age thinks itself the most critical, yet seldom has the clash between light and darkness, good and evil, and truth and falsehood been so obvious, so stark, and so demanding an answer. All around us nations rage, moral foundations are crumbling, and the culture grows increasingly hostile to the Christian faith. The temptation by all too many is to stay silent, to blend in, to soften the message, and to bow quietly so as not to offend. But Christ has not called His people to blend into the background. He has called us to shine as lights in a crooked and perverse generation (Phil 2:15). He has not asked us to be safe, but to be steadfast. He has not asked us to be popular, but to be pure. The Lord is calling forth a remnant, not of the clever or the comfortable, but of the committed. To those who will "Watch, stand fast in the faith, be brave, be strong" (1 Cor 16:13).

Throughout Scripture, God's pattern has never been to win the world with the majority. He saves by the remnant. Gideon's army of 300. Elijah on Mount Carmel against 450 prophets of Baal. Twelve trembling disciples turned into flaming heralds of the gospel. It has never been about numbers but about faithfulness. As Leonard Ravenhill once said, "The world is not waiting for a new definition of the gospel, but for a new demonstration of the power of the gospel."[70] That demonstration will come not from those who compromise, but from those who are courageous enough to take a stand and obey Christ at any cost.

The faithful remnant does not retreat into despair though the day may be dark. They rise with holy determination to act. They are not the elite of the culture but the yielded to Christ. They are not flawless but they are the fearless in their allegiance to the Lord. The question is not whether God will preserve a witness in this age; He always does. The question is whether we will be that witness.

When historians write about the church in the 21st century what will they record? Will they write that we chose to remain silent because we shrank back in fear seeking comfort and cultural approval? Or will they write that we stood tall and bold in the power of the Holy Spirit proclaiming God's eternal truth with love, humility and courage. The next chapter of church history is not being written in dusty libraries by historians; it is being written now, in our homes, in pulpits, in workplaces, in schools and city streets. The ink that is used to write this history is our obedience. The paper is our daily lives. The author is God Himself, yet He has chosen to write His story through the faithful lives of His people. As the Apostle Paul told the Corinthian believers, "You are our epistle written in our hearts, known and read by all men" (2 Cor 3:2).

This is both a sobering responsibility and an exhilarating opportunity. We do not get to choose the times in which we live, but we do get to choose whether we will live faithfully in those times. As A. W. Tozer put it, "A scared world needs a fearless church."[71] This is our call. Not to sit on the sidelines of history wringing our hands as if we are helpless, but to step onto the field of battle, clothed with the full armor of God, and ready to take our stand.

Faithfulness rarely begins with dramatic moments. It begins small in the hidden place. Daniel was faithful in prayer to God long before he faced the edict of King Darius to bow before him. David was faithful with a sling long before he was faithful with Goliath's sword. Paul was faithful in the desert long before he was faithful in the courts of Caesar. The remnant God uses tomorrow is forged in the quiet obedience of today.

Will we be faithful in prayer? Will we be faithful to the Word of God? Will we be faithful in discipling our children in the Lord, in honoring the commitment of our marriages, in loving our neighbors as ourselves, in speaking the truth with love, gentleness, and clarity? These daily choices of faithfulness build the strength of backbone that can withstand great storms. Do not underestimate the power of small acts of obedience because they are the seeds that, in time, can grow into movements that can transform culture.

Staying faithful to God and His Word will mean swimming upstream against the culture. It could mean nasty ridicule, hateful opposition, being slandered and defamed on social media outlets, and perhaps even physical persecution. But this should be no surprise. Jesus told us plainly: "If the world hates you, you know that it hated me before it hated you" (John 15:18). The early believers understood this well. They rejoiced that they were counted worthy to suffer for His name (Acts 5:41). Will we?

We must not think that compromise will shield us and make others embrace us. A church that trims the truth to fit the culture will find itself powerless to change the culture. Salt that loses its savor is good for nothing. Light that is hidden under a bushel benefits no one. This is the hour for Christians to be distinct as God's Word describes. We are not to be arrogant, nor angry, but undeniably different where our lives are clearly marked by the presence of Christ. As Andrew Murray once wrote, "God is ready to assume full responsibility for the life wholly yielded to Him."[72] That is the secret of God's remnant, not their strength, but their surrender.

History testifies that God can turn the world upside down through a few resolute, faithful, and courageous believers. John Wesley once said, "Give me one hundred men who fear nothing but sin and desire nothing but God, and I care not whether they be clergymen or laymen, such alone will shake the gates of hell and set up the kingdom of heaven on earth."[73] That is not empty rhetoric; it has been proven time and again. Revival fires have always begun with small sparks of holy resolve. Nations have been moved, laws have been changed, and cultures have shifted, not because the culture voted its approval, but because God's faithful remnant stood unshaken.

Imagine what God might do through us if we refuse to bow to the culture, if we preach Christ crucified without apology, if we live with the highest integrity when no one is watching, if we love our enemies as ourselves, and pray for those who persecute us. Imagine the witness of a church that uncompromisingly upholds a holy standard, unapologetically stands on the truth of God's Word, and unwaveringly loves others. The world would not be able to ignore that church. The world may oppose it but they would never be able to erase its impact.

At the end of it all, faithfulness is not about making history, but about heeding and following the voice of our Lord. One day every believer will stand before the Lord Jesus Christ, and in that moment, the only words that will truly matter are these: "Well done, good and faithful servant" (Matt 25:23). That is the reward worth living for and worth dying for. Not the applause of the world. Not being at ease in culture. Not relishing in creature comforts. But the smile of our Savior.

The faithful remnant lives with eternity in view. They know there are crowns laid up for those who love His appearing. They know that God's glory far outweighs the sufferings of this present world. They know that heaven is not impressed with numbers but with obedience. They know that history will fade away but the Kingdom of God will endure forever.

So, I ask again: *Will we be found faithful?* Not perfect, but persevering. Not flawless, but fearless. Not sinless, but steadfast. Not cowardly, but courageous. The time for hesitation is over. The time for playing church is past. This is the hour to bend our knees in prayer, to lift our voices in praise, to strengthen our hands for service, and to set our faces like flint toward the mission Christ has given to us to take the gospel to the world and work to renew culture till Jesus comes.

The world does not need another lukewarm generation. It needs believers on fire for God. It needs fathers and mothers raising up children who know the Word of God and love Christ. It needs pastors who will preach with conviction the whole counsel of God and not compromise. It needs young men and women who will dare to go wherever God sends, no matter the cost. It needs ordinary saints living extraordinary faithful lives in the power of the Spirit.

As we reflect on what has been written, let us remember that we are not spectators of history, we are participants. We are not passive observers of America's decline; we are to be salt and light in it. We are not helpless but we are more than conquerors through Him who loved us. And while the world asks, "Where is God?" heaven is asking, "Where are my faithful ones?"

Will we be found faithful? May God grant that the answer to be a resounding YES. Not for our glory, but for His. Not for the applause of men, but for the advance of the gospel. Not so our names are remembered, but so that the name of Jesus is exalted. The next chapter of church history is being written now. And may it be said of us, as it was said of those who came before us: These are they who turned the world upside down (Acts 17:6).

Brothers and sisters, the pen is in God's hand, but the ink in the pen is our faithfulness. Let us rise, let us stand, let us serve, let us suffer, if need be, and let us rejoice that we are counted worthy to bear His name. The story is not finished. The greatest pages may yet be written. By His grace and for His glory, may we be the remnant who will not bow, who will not burn out, and who will not be silent until the whole world knows that Jesus Christ is Lord.

About the Author

Dr. Bob Pearle is a seasoned pastor, theologian, and denominational leader with over four decades of ministry experience. He holds a B.A. in Christian Ministry from Southern Bible College and both the Master of Divinity (1980) and Doctor of Ministry (1992) from Mid-America Baptist Theological Seminary in Cordova, Tennessee.

He has served as President of the Southern Baptists of Texas Convention, as a Trustee of the International Mission Board and LifeWay Christian Resources, and in multiple leadership capacities within Southern Baptist life, including service on the Executive Committee of the Southern Baptists of Texas Convention. His leadership has also extended to trustee roles at Truett McConnell University and Hannibal-LaGrange University.

Dr. Pearle is the author of *The Vanishing Church: Searching for Significance in the 21st Century* (2009) and has served as Pastor of Birchman Baptist Church in Fort Worth, Texas, since 1998. He and his wife, Deborah, have shared fifty-three years of marriage and ministry together.

Notes

[1] "We become more numerous every time we are hewn down by you: the blood of Christians is seed [*Plures efficimur quotiens metimur a vobis; semen est sanguis Christianorum*]." Tertullian and Minucius Felix, *Apologetical Works and Octavius*, ed. Roy Joseph Deferrari, trans. Rudolph Arbesmann, Emily Joseph Daly, and Edwin A. Quain, vol. 10 of *The Fathers of the Church* (Washington, DC: The Catholic University of America Press, 1950), 125 (*Apologeticum* 50.13).

[2] Tertullian, "The Prescription against Heretics," in *Latin Christianity: Its Founder, Tertullian*, ed. Alexander Roberts, James Donaldson, and A. Cleveland Coxe, trans. Peter Holmes, vol. 3 of *The Ante-Nicene Fathers* (Buffalo, NY: Christian Literature Company, 1885), 260 (*De Præscriptione Hæreticorum*, c. 36).

[3] The deaths of the apostles can be found in John Foxe, *Foxe's Book of Martyrs; Being a History of the Persecution of Christians in All Ages* (Philadelphia: Charles Foster Publishing, 1895), 24–35.

[4] Francis X. Glimm, "The Martyrdom of St. Polycarp," in *The Apostolic Fathers*, trans. Francis X. Glimm, Joseph M.-F. Marique, and Gerald G. Walsh, vol. 1 of *The Fathers of the Church* (Washington, DC: The Catholic University of America Press, 1947), 155–56.

[5] Joseph Barber Lightfoot, *The Apostolic Fathers*, ed. J. R. Harmer (London: Macmillan and Co., 1891), 206–208.

[6] See note #1 above. See also William Smith and Henry Wace, eds., "Tertullianus (1), Quintus Septimius Florens," in *A Dictionary of Christian Biography, Literature, Sects and Doctrines* (London: John Murray, 1877–1887), 4:818–64.

[7] Foxe, *Foxe's Book of Martyrs*, 361.

[8] Roland H. Bainton, *Here I Stand: A Life of Martin Luther* (New York: Penguin Books, 1955), 60.

[9] Bainton, *Here I Stand*, 144

[10] F. L. Cross and Elizabeth A. Livingstone, eds., in *The Oxford Dictionary of the Christian Church* (Oxford; New York: Oxford University Press, 2005), 1014.

[11] For this term of reproach, see Leonard Verduin, *The Reformers and Their Stepchildren* (Grand Rapids: Eerdmans, 1964), 189–220.

[12] For the connection between infant baptism and the alliance between church and state, see Leonard Verduin, *The Anatomy of a Hybrid: A Study in Church-State Relationships* (Grand Rapids: Eerdmans, 1976).

[13] William R. Estep Jr., "Thomas Helwys: Bold Architect of Baptist Polity on Church-State Relations," *Baptist History and Heritage* 20.3 (July 1985): 31.

[14] Roger Williams, *The Bloody Tenent of Persecution for Cause of Conscience: Discussed in a Conference between Truth and Peace*, ed. Richard Groves (Macon, GA: Mercer University Press, 2001), 3.

[15] John Winthrop, *The History of New England from 1630 to 1649*, ed. James Savage, 2 vols. (Boston: Little, Brown & Co., 1853), 2:193.

[16] Charlotte Carrington-Farmer, ed., "Rhode Island Charter (1663)," in *Roger Williams and His World: A History in Documents*, ed. by Charlotte Carrington-Farmer, The Broadview Sources Series (Peterborough, Ontario, Canada: Broadview Press, 2025), 80–85.

[17] See Leslie Landrigan, "Obadiah Holmes, The Baptist Martyr the Puritans Should Have Left Alone," *New England Historical Society*, updated 2025, https://newenglandhistoricalsociety.com/obadiah-holmes-baptist-martyr-puritans/; and William Cathcart, *The Baptist Encyclopaedia* […] (Philadelphia: Louis H. Everts, 1881), 538–39.

[18] Cathcart, *The Baptist Encyclopaedia*, 539; Isaac Backus, *A History of New England. With Particular Reference to the Denomination of Christians Called Baptists*, 2nd ed., ed. David Weston, 2 vols. (Newton, MA: The Backus Historical Society, 1871), 1:192.

[19] Wayne E. Thompson and David L. Cummins, *This Day in Baptist History* (Greenville, SC: Bob Jones University Press, 1993), 142.

[20] Cathcart, *The Baptist Encyclopaedia*, 585.

[21] Thompson and Cummins, *This Day in Baptist History*, 66.

[22] Richard D. Land, "John Leland: American patriot and First Amendment hero," *The Christian Post: Voices*, June 21, 2024, https://www.christianpost.com/voices/john-leland-american-patriot-and-first-amendment-hero.html.

[23] Jim Eckman, "The Cultural Accommodation Of American Evangelicals," *Issues in Perspective with Dr. Jim Eckman*, June 22, 2024, https://issuesinperspective.com/2024/06/the-cultural-accommodation-of-american-evangelicals/.

[24] Leonardo Blair, "Loving God and Craft Beer; Churches Combine Beer and Hymns in Rollicking Services to Combat Dwindling Numbers," *The Christian Post* (News), November 4, 2013,

https://www.christianpost.com/news/loving-god-and-craft-beer-churches-combine-beer-and-hymns-in-rollicking-services-to-combat-dwindling-numbers.html.

[25] SBC, "Resolution on Abortion: 1971 Annual Meeting," *SBC.net* (Resources), June 1, 1971, https://www.sbc.net/resource-library/resolutions/resolution-on-abortion-2/.

[26] SBC, "Resolution on Abortion and Sanctity of Human Life: 1974 Annual Meeting," *SBC.net* (Resources), June 1, 1974, https://www.sbc.net/resource-library/resolutions/resolution-on-abortion-and-sanctity-of-human-life/.

[27] SBC, "Resolution on Abortion: 1976 Annual Meeting," *SBC.net* (Resources), June 1, 1976, https://www.sbc.net/resource-library/resolutions/resolution-on-abortion-3/.

[28] See Ps 139:13–16 and Jer 1:5.

[29] SBC, "Resolution on Abortion: 1980 Annual Meeting," *SBC.net* (Resources), June 1, 1980, https://www.sbc.net/resource-library/resolutions/resolution-on-abortion-6/.

[30] See 2 Cor 5:17.

[31] Ryan Foley, "American Bible Society survey finds 'unprecedented drop' in Bible reading," *The Christian Post* (News), April 7, 2022, https://www.christianpost.com/news/american-bible-society-finds-unprecedented-drop-in-bible-users-report.html.

[32] George Barna, "Survey on Adult Churchgoers on Social Issues and Worldview: A National Survey from the Center for Biblical Worldview," *Center for Biblical Worldview* (June 2023): 3, https://downloads.frc.org/EF/EF23H29.pdf.

[33] David F. Wells, *God in the Wasteland: The Reality of Truth in a World of Fading Dreams* (Grand Rapids: Eerdmans, 1994), 88.

[34] Philip Rieff, *The Triumph of the Therapeutic: Uses of Faith After Freud* (Chicago: University of Chicago Press, 1966).

[35] Christian Smith and Melinda Lundquist Denton, *Soul Searching: The Religious and Spiritual Lives of American Teenagers* (Oxford: Oxford University Press, 2005), 162–71.

[36] David F. Wells, *No Place for Truth: Or Whatever Happened to Evangelical Theology?* (Grand Rapids: Eerdmans, 1993), 183.

[37] Carl R. Trueman, *The Rise and Triumph of the Modern Self* (Wheaton: Crossway, 2020), 46.

[38] D. Martyn Lloyd-Jones, *Authority* (Edinburgh: Banner of Truth, 1984), 56.

[39] Ryan Foley, "Churches failing to preach about sin is a 'bodyblow' as many Christians reject basic teachings: Barna," *The Christian Post* (News), September 6, 2025, https://www.christianpost.com/news/barna-calls-churches-failure-to-preach-about-sin-a-bodyblow.html.

[40] Foley, "Churches failing to preach about sin," https://www.christianpost.com/news/barna-calls-churches-failure-to-preach-about-sin-a-bodyblow.html.

[41] Gregory A. Smith, et al., "About Three-in-Ten U.S. Adults Are Now Religiously Unaffiliated," *Pew Research Center*, December 14, 2021, https://www.pewresearch.org/religion/2021/12/14/about-three-in-ten-u-s-adults-are-now-religiously-unaffiliated/.

[42] This quote is widely attributed to Spurgeon, though it is spurious. What is likely the case is that it has evolved from sermons and writings of Archibald Geikie Brown (1844–1922), a Calvinistic Baptist minister and a student, a friend, and an associate of Spurgeon. Brown was the pastor of the Metropolitan Tabernacle in London from 1908–1911, the church earlier pastored by Spurgeon.

[43] Dwight Randall, "Bill Hybels' Frank Admission About 'Seeker Friendly' Churches," *Life Ministries: Helping Build the Church*, May 6, 2008, https://lifeministries.org.au/bill-hybels-frank-admission-seeker-friendly-churches/.

[44] Dietrich Bonhoeffer, *Dietrich Bonhoeffer: Letters and Papers from Prison*, ed. Eberhard Bethge (New York: Touchtone, 1997), 14.

[45] Eric Metaxas, *Bonhoeffer: Pastor, Martyr, Prophet, Spy* (Nashville: Thomas Nelson, 2010), 532.

[46] See "Martyrdom in Ecuador: 'Go Ye and Preach the Gospel'—Five Do and Die," *Life* 40, no. 5 (January 30, 1956): 10–19, https://archive.org/details/Life-1956-01-30-Vol-40-No-5/page/n11/mode/2up.

[47] Jim Elliot, *The Journals of Jim Elliot*, ed. Elisabeth Elliot (Grand Rapids: Revell, 1978), 174.

[48] Elisabeth Elliot, *Through the Gates of Splendor* (1957; repr., Carol Stream, IL: Tyndale House, 1986).

[49] Steve Saint, *End of the Spear* (Carol Stream, IL: Tyndale House, 2005).

[50] Douglas Sweeney, *The American Evangelical Story: A History of the Movement* (Grand Rapids: Baker Academic, 2005), 196–97.

[51] Martin Luther King, Jr., *Letter from Birmingham Jail*, April 16, 1963.

[52] Aleksandr Solzhenitsyn, *Nobel Lecture in Literature* (Stockholm: The Nobel Foundation, 1970).

[53] Aleksandr Solzhenitsyn, "A World Split Apart," Harvard Commencement Address, June 8, 1978.

[54] Misty Bernall, *She Said Yes: The Unlikely Martyrdom of Cassie Bernall* (Farmington, PA: Plough Publishing, 1999).

[55] Beth Nimmo and Darrell Scott, *Rachel's Tears: The Spiritual Journey of Columbine Martyr Rachel Scott* (Nashville: Thomas Nelson, 2000).

[56] Jack Phillips, *The Cost of My Faith: How a Decision in My Cake Shop Took Me to the Supreme Court* (Washington, D.C.: Salem Books, 2021), 5.

[57] Gilbert Keith Chesterton, *What's Wrong with the World* (New York: Dodd, Mead and Company, 1910), 48.

[58] Victoria Barnett, *For the Soul of the People: Protestant Protest Against Hitler* (Oxford: Oxford University Press, 1992).

[59] Taylor Branch, *Parting the Waters: America in the King Years, 1954–63* (Simon & Schuster, 1988).

[60] Richard Wurmbrand, *Tortured for Christ* (London: Hayfield Publishing Co., 1967).

[61] Eric Metaxas, *Bonhoeffer: Pastor, Martyr, Prophet, Spy* (Thomas Nelson, 2010). For the reported quote ("the words have never been directly traced to Bonhoeffer") that is more likely a summation of what Bonhoeffer taught, see p. xxiv.

[62] GCR Conversation, "Why Andrew Brunson Never Heard from God in Prison," *Global Christian Relief*, September 7, 2021, https://globalchristianrelief.org/stories/why-andrew-brunson-never-heard-from-god-in-prison/.

[63] Leonard Ravenhill, *Why Revival Tarries* (1987; repr., Minneapolis: Bethany House, 2004), 27.

[64] A.W. Tozer, *The Dwelling Place of God* (Chicago: Moody Publishers, 2015), 23.

[65] Andrew Murray, *The Inner Chamber and the Inner Life* (New Kensington, PA: Whitaker House, 1989), 45.

[66] Max Lucado, *The Great House of God: A Home for Your Heart* (Nashville: Thomas Nelson, 2011), 46.

[67] O. Hallesby, *Prayer* (Minneapolis: Fortress Press, 1994), 152.

[68] Ravenhill, *Why Revival Tarries*, 19.

[69] A. W. Tozer, *The Root of the Righteous* (Chicago: Moody Publishers, 2015), 7.

[70] Ravenhill, *Why Revival Tarries*, 121.

[71] A.W. Tozer, *The Tozer Pulpit: Selections from His Sermons* (Camp Hill, PA: WingSpread Publishers, 2009), 27.

[72] Andrew Murray, *The Believer's Secret of Waiting on God* (Springdale, PA: Whitaker House, 1987), 18.
[73] John Wesley, *The Journal of John Wesley* (Chicago: Moody Press, 1951), 216.

www.ingramcontent.com/pod-product-compliance
Lightning Source LLC
Chambersburg PA
CBHW071117090426
42736CB00012B/1934